In the Company of Friends

Dreamwork within a Sufi Group

Llewellyn Vaughan-Lee

First published in the United States in 1994 by
The Golden Sufi Center
P.O. Box 428, Inverness, California 94937

Cover Design by Tennessee Dixon.
Printed and Bound by McNaughton & Gunn
using recycled paper.

Library of Congress Cataloging in Publication Data,
Vaughan-Lee, Llewellyn
In the Company of Friends:
Dreamwork within a Sufi Group
1. Spiritual life
2. Dreams—Religious aspects
3. Sufism

Library of Congress Catalog Card Number: 93-81052
ISBN 0-9634574-1-1

Contents

Preface

Throughout this book, in an effort to maintain continuity and simplicity of text, the masculine pronoun is used for both the seeker and the teacher. Similarly, God, the Great Beloved, is referred to as He. Of course, the Absolute Truth is neither masculine nor feminine. As much as It has a divine masculine side, so It has an awe-inspiring feminine aspect.

The dogs bark, the caravan passes by.
Sufi saying

Go, oh heart, go with the caravan!
Go not alone over the stages of the way.
Rûmî

Introduction

Many wonders are manifest in sleep:
in sleep the heart becomes a window.
One that is awake and dreams beautiful dreams,
he is the knower of God. Receive the dust of his eyes.

Rûmî[1]

Dreams come from the unknown. Sometimes they retell the images of our daily life or lead us down confused corridors. But some dreams speak with the voice of the soul. They have a quality, a music, a depth of feeling that belong to the sacred part of ourself. They open a hidden door into a beyond that is also the most intimate part of our inner being.

Listening to these dreams we can hear the voice of our deeper self. Speaking to us in its own language, a language of images, symbols, and feelings, a dream can guide us through the tortuous maze of our psyche. As both teacher and guide, these dreams are of infinite value on the inner journey. They call us inward into the mystery and wonder that is our real nature. When the body is asleep, when our everyday life has laid down its burdens, these dreams tell us of another world and of a winding pathway that can lead us into the depths.

From the beginning of our quest our dreams tell of both the treasures and the dangers that await the homeward traveller. Dreams have always been the messengers of the gods, and they entice us inward, away from the desert of our material culture, towards the oasis of the soul. Dreams are both messengers and manna, pointing out the path and feeding the needy traveller with the numinous substance of his inner self. They provide encouragement, wonder, direction, beauty, and also terror. In our dreams we both encounter our inner demons and are awakened to our hidden center, glimpsing a vista on which the sun of the Self never sets.

Asleep we can easily enter into the reality of dreams and fully experience its intensity. But when we open our eyes its landscapes fade, its wonder slips away. Only too easily does the harsh light of the outer world dissolve this inner beauty, and then we are unable to grasp its poignant message or to taste its nourishment. In our Western culture the outer world seems to have little place for the symbolic wisdom of our dreams. The demands of our everyday life draw a heavy curtain that obscures our endless inner horizons. As we awaken into a regulated world of time and space the scent of the soul is forgotten. Our dreams then remain just a forgotten interlude in a demanding, competitive world, whose material values have no place for the intangible secrets we have heard whispered in the night.

It is easy to say, "Follow your dreams, listen to their wisdom and allow them to guide you." But what if we cannot clearly hear the story they tell us? What if the subtlety of their music is lost in the clamor of the outer world? We live in a culture that has lost contact with the soul and is no longer nourished by its dreams. As children we are told not to dream but to pay attention to the outer world. As we grow up we enter an adult world whose addiction to material progress has been bought at the price of the inner world.

The outer world and our collective conditioning batter our ability to listen to our dreams. Our inner ear is bombarded with the denser "dreams" of material prosperity. It is only too easy to miss the intangible thread that is the guidance offered by the soul's dreams. And without knowing it we can close off the doorway that stands at the threshold of sleep. Imprisoned in the collective values of the present time we remain a stranger to our real self.

In older, more "primitive" cultures, when an individual had an important dream he or she would go to the shaman or holy man of the tribe. The shaman would listen to the dream and intuit its meaning. In this way the message and energy of the dream would be valued and integrated into the life of the dreamer. In some cases if it was an important dream the whole tribe would be called to enact it. The collective would be nourished by the dream and not regard it as a mere fantasy. Dreams and everyday life were seen as complementary rather than opposite.

Today our outer life is starved by the lack of meaning, meaning that can only come from within. Drug and alcohol addictions point to the need for non-material nourishment, yet the collective is still entranced by the shallow delights of material progress. We need the nourishment and guidance of our dreams, but we do not have easy access to a shaman and our neighbors and colleagues will rarely enact our dreams. For some people their therapist or analyst takes the role of the shaman, and can function as a helpful intermediary to the unconscious. But the therapeutic relationship often focuses on the resolution of problems rather than the development of a natural opening to the inner world. Furthermore the financial expense of analysis or therapy limits its availability. The shaman, respected and supported by the tribe, is a very different figure from today's therapist.

There are individuals strong enough to withstand alone the pressures of the collective. Driven by a destiny that does not allow them to "fit in" they follow their deeper need at whatever the cost. These solitary individuals are often unnoticed, their journey unreported. A few are visible as great pioneers like Galileo, Saint Theresa of Avila, or Carl Jung. Whether forgotten or remembered, these individuals cannot be pressured or conditioned to surrender their dreams. They must live their vision, follow their lonely and relentless path. But not all seekers have this tremendous strength. Most of us need outer support in order to follow our inner vision. We need a container to protect our dreams against the pressures of the collective.

One type of container that can provide a secure link between the individual's inner world and the outer world is a group. Any group of people that places value on the inner world and recognizes the individual's ability to gain access to his or her own inner wisdom can be a sacred space where the two worlds meet. In such a group both healing and transformation can take place. Here individuals are able to open to the energies of the inner world and allow these energies to flow into the outer world where there is such need for them.

In the Company of Friends is an exploration of the way a group can function both as a support for individuals making their own inner journey and as a container of spiritual energy. This book is based upon my own personal experience with a Sufi group, but the ideas presented are not limited to this tradition. Any group that meets together for inner work can function as a sacred space. The essential dynamic of such a group is that the individuals meet together for the purpose of transformation beyond the ego. If a group meets for this purpose the group is both energized and protected by the Self, the source and the goal of our inner drive for transformation.

The energy of the Self, "That boundless power, source of every power,"[2] can create a link between the inner and outer worlds that is not contaminated by the thought-forms or pressures of the collective. It contains the individual within the sphere of greatest potential. "Maker of past and future," the Self offers the possibility for each of us to realize our own essence and also make our maximum contribution to life.

Individuals are attracted to groups with which they have an inner harmony, as expressed in the *hadîth* (saying attributed to the Prophet), "souls make cohorts; they form in groups according to their chosen affinities."[3] For some individuals the group to which they are attracted may have a distinct spiritual orientation; it may be Buddhist, Christian, Sufi, or another spiritual path. Some groups may be formed around a particular teacher while others may be focused on a set of teachings. Groups can also be composed of individuals drawn together for dreamwork or other forms of inner exploration.

Whatever the outer form, it is the inner attitude of the individuals that determines the dynamic and potential for transformation offered by the group. The more the individuals are focused on the Self and committed to the work of self-transformation, the more the energy of the Self permeates the group. The desire for Truth, the desire to realize one's inner being, *attracts the energy of the Self*, as expressed in Christ's words, "When two or three are gathered together in my name, there I am in the midst of them."[4] If two or more people in a group have a deep desire for Truth they will form an inner core of commitment through which the energy of the Self can be channelled to help those whose desire for Truth is less strong. Sincere aspiration gives nourishment not just to the individual but to the whole group and beyond. Channelling the energy of the Self, such a group becomes a point of light, bringing the nourishment and wholeness of the Self into the world of time and space.

Weaving together dreams and spiritual stories, *In the Company of Friends* traces a thread in which the group plays a central role. Following this thread, this book explores many aspects of the homeward journey: the pain of Truth, the opening of the heart, our natural state of prayer, the purpose of pain, and the intimacies of love. On this ancient journey of the soul we each make our own individual way and yet we are walking a path that is humanity's most primal dream. Totally alone we are in the company of all those who have gone before us and all those whose longing draws them, too, back to the center of themselves. In this company we are held in the hearts of the friends of God.

THROUGH A GLASS DARKLY

For now we see through a glass, darkly;
but then face to face: now I know in part;
but then shall I know even as I am known.
Saint Paul[1]

THE GOLDEN THREAD

Dreams tell stories. They are the stories of our inner life, the tales of our unconscious self, our fears and hopes, despairs and loves. Like fairground mirrors they offer different pictures of ourself, seeming distortions of both beauty and horror. Sometimes we are chased down endless corridors, sometimes we meet the lover we long for. Always our dreams point behind the façade of the world, revealing other faces than those we show to our friends and colleagues.

But amidst the seeming distortions of our dreams, in the myriad reflections they offer us, a single thread is hidden. This thread is our own story; not the story of our outer life, but the deeper destiny of our own being. It is the story of the soul going Home, the search for the invisible treasure which is nothing other than our own essence.

In the outer world we are continually distracted, caught and confused by our desires, by the responsibilities, difficulties, and attractions of everyday life. But when we sleep the outer world disappears. We are free to forget its illusions. We are free to hear the voice of our own longing as it speaks to us in our dreams, telling us the stories of our innermost self, a self we ave often forgotten and disowned. When we awake the dream remains as a reminder, pointing our way along the path. It carries with it the energy of the inner world, the scent of the garden of the soul. The work then is to make the dream real: to integrate its energy into consciousness and make its story a part of our life.

Following our dreams, watching their images and listening to their music—this work is a process of attunement, attuning our consciousness to our own mystery, the heartbeat of our own soul. And as we listen to our dreams, so they share their secret; they point to this golden thread that is the innermost dream. This dream is the soul's one message: the spiritual purpose of our life which is the journey Home. The golden thread connects us to the source, that place deep within the heart where Truth is waiting. And as we follow this thread, slowly we see that behind every reflection, behind every masked face, whether lover or tyrant, is our own face. This is not the face that we show to the world or even show to ourself. It does not belong to the ego or the personality, but is hinted at by our dreams. Both unknown and familiar it is "the face we had before we were born."

As we watch our dreams we sense this essential aspect of our being. Unknowingly we feel the attraction, and hear the call from the depths to "return to the root of the root of your own self." Opening to our dreams we open an inner eye which can trace the golden thread of our own unique spiritual path. Slowly this thread becomes clearer, more distinct. We attune ourself to its subtleties, learn to listen to the guidance it offers. It calls to us, and, responding, we look inward, gradually glimpsing the profound purpose of our life. In this way our destiny comes to meet us and our sense of alienation dissolves. We become familiar with our own essence.

DREAMWORK

To work with dreams is to work with the symbolic substance that underlies our life. The images and symbols that come to us in dreams are not idle fantasies, but point to a reality that is deeper than the reality of the outer world. Almost all processes of inner growth and transformation depend upon working with this symbolic stratum of the psyche. It forms the embryo from which we are reborn.

Dreamwork can take many forms, and each of us learns to work with our dreams in our own way; we learn to make our own intimate relationship with our symbolic nature. Some dreams remain as an enigma, reminding us that we are deeper than logic and more profound than the mind can grasp. As we bring these dreams into our waking life we allow their mystery to be infused into the ordinary world, blurring the borders with which we delineate ourself. Their subtle impact upon our consciousness reminds us that the unknown is always greater than the known. Their energy permeates the protective boundaries we have erected, gradually breaking down the walls that hide our consciousness from the infinite inner world.

Medieval sailors stayed close to the shore, for on their maps the deeper seas were charted with unknown dangers. Voyaging beyond the horizon one could fall off the edge of the world. Twentieth-century conditioning has charted the inner world with similar warnings. We are advised to stay close to the shore and keep our attention focused on the known land of consciousness, the towns and cities of our rational civilization. But just as the pull of the unknown forced the mariners to sail beyond the horizon, into those seas marked "Here there be dragons," so do our dreams bring disquieting and exciting news of real adventures and fantastic mythical creatures. When a friend dreamt that a wounded unicorn flew to her asking for help, she was confronted by a dimension of herself that was both miraculous and frightening.

The inner world comes to us in our dreams because it needs our attention. It is not a problem to be solved but a part of our self that needs to be accepted and understood. Carl Jung wrote, "A dream that is not understood remains a mere occurrence; understood it becomes a living experience." We need to make our dream world into a living experience, because only then can we be nurtured by its magic. This magic is our own essence, which the walls of our rational culture have shut out and banished. Dreamwork helps us to make this magic real, and so enables us to be nourished by the manna that we need on our journey Home.

A SPIRITUAL CONTEXT FOR DREAMWORK

In the Sufi tradition we share dreams within a group, which is an important complement to individual dreamwork. Ultimately it is for the dreamer to feel the substance of his dream and integrate its meaning into consciousness. But sharing dreams within a group can greatly help this process, not just for the dreamer but for all those who are participating.

When dreams are shared within a space made sacred through meditation and aspiration, their inner core and deepest meaning become more visible, more accessible to consciousness. Through meditation the space is cleared of many of the thought-forms that distract us from our inner work. And at the same time meditation aligns the group with the Self and with the whole process of the journey Home. Thus the song of the soul can be heard more clearly and consciousness can be open to the mystery of a dream. In this way the energy of the group "opens" the dream, enabling its symbols to be more translucent. It is as if the journey itself within the listeners welcomes the dream that is being told.

This journey is not just a path we walk or a route we take, but a living substance of the soul, a spiritual energy that we need to bring into our daily life. This is the esoteric meaning of Christ's saying, "I am the way, the truth and the life."[2] In the depths of the psyche there is a substance that is both the pilgrim and the path, and one of the experiences that the wayfarer encounters is the realization that he or she is the path, that the spiritual journey does not take you anywhere, but is an unveiling of our inner essence. I once had a dream in which the teacher was leading me and the group away from a children's school round and round in circles. In the dream I was annoyed that we were not being led anywhere, but when I awoke I realized that the dream's message was that there is nowhere to go. At the beginning, in the "children's school" of the dream, there is the idea of a spiritual quest or journey that takes us from one place to another. Later we have to let go of that illusion, and instead allow our inner essence to unfold into our life. The journey is like an inward spiral that takes us deeper and deeper, until finally both the journey and the traveller vanish and only His presence remains. In the center of the spiral there is the final mystery of our nonexistence.

The Self hidden in the depths of the unconscious calls to us and we respond, turning inward, seeking what we have lost. Our dreams guide us, outlining the path, pointing us deeper, giving us glimpses of the mystery He has hidden within us. The journey is endless because we are endless. It is an opening into our own infinite nature. In the following dream the dreamer hopes to have arrived somewhere, but even the sense of direction dissolves into a greater horizon:

> With a small group of people I am climbing up a steep mountain. We are equipped with mountain boots, but no safety rope. I look around me and realize that this mountain is completely vertical, then I go on climbing up. Having with relief reached the top, I glance around and all I can see is a vast landscape of hills covered with trees, forest, and more hills! Oh no … and which direction?

The journey is a living presence that dissolves the frontiers of our consciousness, enabling us to slowly merge into the limitless dimension of our own being. The journey leads us into the eternal present, and at the same time it is the eternal present coming to meet us. It is both the call of the Self and our response to this call. It leads us from the mind, which functions in duality—our mind registers through contrast and comparison—to the heart, which embraces us in the oneness of love. Thus at the beginning we understand this process of inner transformation from a mental perspective as a journey which leads us from one place to another, but slowly love dissolves the mind and the journey becomes a meeting in which we are immersed deeper and deeper until finally we become lost in the vast oneness of the heart.

This living presence we call the journey resonates to the inner mysteries expressed in dreams, and this resonance creates a state within the group in which the dreams allow themselves to unfold more completely. Dreams are not bound by the strict logic of the mind, and are thus able to introduce our consciousness to inner realities which can appear paradoxical. The receptive psyche of the group allows this quality of a dream to be held and fostered, rather than attacked by the thought-forms and fears of the rational mind. Dream reality is very elusive and easily overshadowed by the denser nature of the material world. And just as you cannot appreciate a painting in a room cluttered with refuse, neither can you sense the meaning of a dream in an environment that is not sympathetic. This is particularly important in dreams that direct us into the often disturbing realm of the spirit. Dreams that tell of the security that only lies in total insecurity need to be heard in a space inwardly aligned to this process.

The following dream tells the simple story of a pending execution which from a spiritual perspective is highly auspicious. It was dreamt by a man the night before he came to a Sufi group for the first time:

> Seven men have been sentenced to death, to be shot in the head. The judge is in the next room and although there is the possibility of a pardon he is not interested in giving it.

The dreamer awoke from this dream in a very disturbed state. But when he told the dream within the group it was welcomed as the song of a soul going Home. The image of being shot in the head points to a journey beyond the mind, while the whole theme of an execution images the death of the ego. This death is the sacrifice that makes us love's willing slave, and allows us to live in the presence of the Beloved. Rûmî joyfully tells us of this lovers' bargain:

I would love to kiss you.
And the price of this kissing is your life.

Now my love is running towards my life shouting,
What a bargain, let's buy it. ³

The Sufi seeks to "die before we die," to transcend the ego while still living in this world. The real executioner is always the Beloved into whose Hands the lover gives his whole being. Only the Beloved can hold the heart and cut the threads that attach it to the world, though the sheikh, or teacher, as someone who is already "dead," who is surrendered to God, is able to play the part of executioner. Bahâ ad-dîn Naqshband, the founder of the Naqshbandi Order, was said to have had the position of executioner at the court of a ruler of Bukhârâ; and Irina Tweedie would often refer to her Sufi master, Bhai Sahib, as her beloved executioner.

Spiritual values are often the direct opposite of worldly values. When the dreamer awoke from his dream of a pending execution he was threatened by images whose meaning he did not understand. But when he told it within the group its deepest meaning could be contained and affirmed. He was given the opportunity to appreciate the dream's auspicious and unambiguous message.

THE GROUP AS A CONTAINER

The group was able to provide a context for this dream and help the dreamer understand its transformative potential. But the dreamwork happens not just on a mental level, not just on the level of interpretation. There is an inner dynamic in which the group psyche responds to the dream, affirming its potency to the psyche of the dreamer and providing a container to help him integrate it into consciousness.

In therapy or analysis it is the relationship between the therapist and the client that provides the alchemical vessel that contains the inner work. Without this container the client would not feel secure enough to uncover whatever difficulties or vulnerabilities lie at the source of the problem. This sense of security happens primarily at an unconscious level—the psyche of the client feels safe. The same process happens within a group in that the group is a psychological container for the dreamwork. It is this sense of security that enables the psyche of the dreamer to open and become more accessible to consciousness.

For the psyche the greatest sense of security is given by the energy of the Self. Although the Self may be threatening to the mind and to ego-consciousness, for the psyche it provides the ultimate security. It is the rock that is the foundation of our psychic structure. Thus the more a group is attuned with the energy of the Self, the greater the sense of security that is experienced. This enables a quality and depth of dreamwork to take place that reflect the spiritual orientation of the group.

However, the security offered by the energy of the Self is directly opposite to any concept of ego-security. The Self offers an inner security that is absolute and not relative, and is based upon detachment rather than attachment. It is not dependent upon emotional or material well-being, but rather an inner state of poverty. This attitude of spiritual poverty is reflected in a Sufi saying: "Only that which cannot be lost in a shipwreck is yours," and of course in a shipwreck you can lose even your life. Security for the Self is insecurity for the ego.

The group's alignment to the energy of the Self provides an inner foundation for the work of self-transformation whose goal is to transcend the ego. Yet because at the same time this energy can be destabilizing and destructive to the ego patterns that often appear to offer people security, it can make a Sufi group inwardly dangerous because the unconscious dynamic is directed towards destroying both outer and inner attachments. Somebody once flew across America to come to our group, only to run away after a few minutes. She sensed the dynamic emptiness at the core of the group and it terrified her.

Many people are attracted to "spiritual" groups for the sense of a collective security based upon inner attachments rather than inner freedom. The collective psychological patterns that bond a group together can often be forms of co-dependence or shared shadow-projection. Co-dependence is essentially a collective insecurity in which the individuals do not have to stand on their own feet but are rather supported by the group dynamic. In some instances this group dynamic can be the collective adherence to a charismatic leader to whom the members of the group surrender their individual will. A shared shadow-projection is most obvious in politics in which one party believes itself to be right and all others wrong. This reaches a dangerous extreme in religious fanaticism when the group coheres around the notion that only the followers of a particular ideology are to be saved. Psychologically this creates a co-dependence in which the individual's sense of self-worth comes from belonging to the "chosen ones."

However, if a group has the energy of the Self at its central core then the participants are continually thrown back upon themselves, and are not allowed to become dependent upon anything other than the Self. The Self pulls us inward to our essence which is hidden in the unconscious. It focuses us upon our individual inner journey. The Self is tremendously dynamic and can be understood as a spinning center or "pole." The nature of this spinning is that it throws off impurities and only at the center is there any stability. Those who seek the security that only comes with total insecurity are attracted to this center, while others find the energy too disturbing and leave the group.

ISOLATION AND THE COLLECTIVE SHADOW

There is another important unconscious dynamic in a meditation group which is that the group psyche collectively values the inner process. This happens on an individual level in the analytic encounter, in which something so elusive and insubstantial as psychological transformation is recognized and honored. This very act of honoring the inner process helps to bridge the chasm between the conscious and the unconscious that is one of the greatest and most dangerous wounds of our society. But within a group this affirmation happens on a collective level which provides an important counterbalance to our Western collective denial of the inner world and collective assertion that only the outer material world has value. The presence of fellow wayfarers helps us to realize the significance of our inner longing, and protects us from a social environment that is inhospitable to the inward nature of the journey.

In particular, a spiritual group can help us with the feelings of isolation and alienation that burden almost all spiritual travellers. The ego does not choose the process of self-transformation. It is written in the destiny of the soul and activated in response to the call of the Self. When the moment is right the Self, hidden in the unconscious, calls to us and begins to turn our attention away from the outer world towards the innermost secret place, the heart of hearts. It is a lonely journey, "from the alone to the Alone," and even before this journey is activated it can create a sense of isolation within the individual. Often from childhood we have the feeling that we do not "fit in," and may even overcompensate for this feeling by trying extra hard to be socially acceptable. We enact the story of the ugly duckling until we fall into the company of fellow travellers and begin to see our real nature.

This instinctual feeling of alienation is easily overlaid by the collective shadow of a culture which rejects the inner journey. Not only do we carry the loneliness of our own inner journey, but we also feel this collective rejection, without necessarily knowing what it is. We feel that something essential is not allowed, and just as children blame themselves for their parents' problems, we can easily feel that it is all our fault. Our isolation becomes intensified. On an external level we may be socially adapted, but our true nature is caught in this double shadow.

For those who are destined to be inwardly awakened, this journey is like a stamp imprinted in the core of our being. But the inner journey is rejected by the collective, and because this journey is an essential part of our being, we feel the pain of the collective rejection. Yet the sense of social isolation in fact paradoxically comes from being inwardly connected. It is because we are not able to reject the inner world that we cannot "fit in" with a culture dedicated to external material values. Unlike the culture that surrounds us, we are not totally disconnected. It is because of this that we are able to feel the pull of the Self that leads us into the inner world.

Yet as a result of this inner connection we may also feel the pain of the rejected inner world itself. It is not only consciousness that is wounded by the experience of separation. The inner world is also wounded and calls to us for help. Ultimately we do not make the inner journey for ourself. In the work of our own transformation we bring light into the depths of the inner world. And it is because we feel the pain of the inner world that we are able to respond.

But we need a container for this work. For most of us it is too difficult to confront the collective pain of our culture and at the same time experience our own wounds and sense of isolation, without the security and company of friends, of fellow seekers. A group can be a wonderful container for psychological and spiritual work.

Our sense of isolation may not only be rooted in the unconscious, but may be painfully alive in these hidden depths. The unconscious is not just a storehouse of memories but a living organism that is usually more sensitive than our conscious self. The figures that come to us in our dreams are not abstract images but aspects of our own inner self which often carry a sensitivity that we do not allow into our conscious life. Adapting to collective social norms we repress our sensitivity together with our instinctual and creative drives. Repressed into the unconscious these aspects of our self do not just lie dormant, but often feel the pain of rejection.

In our extroverted, materialistic culture the inner desire to return Home is easily repressed into the darkness where it feels the pain of both a personal and a collective alienation. When we are hurt or rejected we tend to retreat further into ourself. The same is true of aspects of our inner self. Our spiritual longing, feeling the pain of rejection, can bury itself even deeper into the unconscious, making it even more inaccessible to consciousness. The split between the conscious and the unconscious easily grows greater.

But in the presence of a group of sincere seekers, this primal desire for Truth feels welcomed. When a person first comes to our group his psyche often rejoices at this acceptance and responds with a series of dreams or an unexpected feeling of joy. It need no longer be covered with guilt because it does not "fit in" to what is socially acceptable. There may be a profound feeling of confirmation as what had been unacceptable and misunderstood is recognized for its true potential. The quest hidden within the heart of the seeker can tell its story of the wonders that are waiting, of execution, death, and rebirth.

Shared within a group the inner journey need no longer carry the shame of being a social outcast. It is no longer a secret that has to be hidden even from the traveller because of the rejection that it fears. It is the group psyche that can offer this sense of acceptance. The psyche of the group speaks to the psyche of the individual and the greatest sense of reassurance happens at an unconscious level. Consciously a person may feel a sense of relief, sensing that something deep within is recognized and does not have to be denied. But often it is the unconscious that responds and opens to this new environment while consciousness is still caught in old patterns of defense. The unconscious is both more sensitive and more flexible than consciousness.

It can happen that a dream suddenly demands to be told, despite the reticence of the dreamer. A woman who had no conscious desire to acknowledge that she was a seeker found to her surprise that she was telling the following dream:

> I am flying over a landscape full of comfortable suburban houses. I long to be down there, in this landscape, but at the same time I feel a far greater pull to fly towards the distant horizon.

This dream describes in straightforward imagery a conflict within the dreamer that is familiar to many of us. The desire for an "ordinary" life is overshadowed by this pull of the unknown. We long to be like other people who are not tormented by the quest for the beyond, who are not driven into the abyss of themselves.

It is not easy to consciously accept the stamp of the quest, because we know in our depths the price we must pay. Even for those who are introverts and natural loners, one of the most bitter pills is the terrible aloneness that befalls the traveller. We have to walk alone on the path to the beyond. It is "as narrow as the edge of the razor"and two cannot walk side by side. The relationship with Truth or God is one to one. God is a jealous lover and He does not allow our hearts to be turned towards anyone other than Him; in the words of al-Hallâj, "Solitary, God loves only the solitary—One, He loves only he who witnesses Him as One."[4]

The journey Home demands that we leave behind everything that separates us from our inner essence. Irina Tweedie describes how desolate the landscape can appear:

It is a lonely path. It is as if you are standing on a high mountain, your feet in the snow, the storms of the mountains whistling around your ears, and down in the valley you see people playing with toys, there is laughter and fun. You feel like saying, "Come, see what is here, leave all that illusion." But what can you offer, cold feet, storms, and the cold wind? But the sky is dark like ink and you are near God.[5]

Embarking on this journey, do you want to leave behind all your friends, everything that is familiar? Do you want to sit alone and cry for the Beloved until your tears have washed away all the past? But is there anything more worthwhile?

THE TASTE OF TRUTH

In *The Conference of the Birds* 'Attâr tells the story of an Arab who falls in with a group of Sufis called Qalanders. They have nothing but muddy wine and they invite the Arab into their dwelling. They give him a glass of wine and he loses his senses. They take everything from him, his gold and silver and all his possessions, and giving him more wine leave him in the street. When he returns home his companions ask him what happened, but he says that he doesn't know except that he was parted from his possessions and now he has nothing. He met a group of Qalanders who just said to him the one word: "Enter."

A friend had a dream that told a similar story. She had this dream before she came to our group for the first time, as if her unconscious was trying to warn her. In fact on her actual physical journey to the group her car was broken into and her valuables were stolen, while her sister's possessions which were also in the car were not touched!

A man and a woman, a married couple, are visiting a community of people who are isolated from the outside world. They have been invited.

Each becomes independently aware of a foreboding feeling regarding these people. There is something strange about them. Although for some reason they are unable to discuss their foreboding openly with one another, they each separately come to the decision that these people are evil and that they mean to kill the couple in some kind of ritual way and to drink their blood and eat their hearts. They are not perfectly sure, but the couple remark on the fact that they are served wine but the others do not drink the wine. When one of the couple naïvely asks why are only they being served wine at this meal, which is outside under the trees, meaningful looks are exchanged among their hosts. This is really when the foreboding turns into a certainty. Someone giggles unpleasantly and says, "Oh, we have our own wine to drink." Everybody then chuckles knowingly. The couple each come to the conclusion that it is their blood which will be the wine. The wife wonders if her husband is aware and fears he is not. But he is as cognizant as she and he realizes that the wine is drugged.

Then they are being taken away to wait until the time of the ritual, and while they are walking through some desert area they manage to escape and run off into the countryside. At the end of

> the dream the couple are terribly frightened.
> They are being pursued and feel that they might
> be able to get away but they are not sure.

In this dream there is a sense of evil and foreboding. Who are these people who are going to drink the couple's blood as wine? What is the nature of this ultimate sacrifice? From the perspective of the ego the spiritual path is destruction and death. It is a terrible undertaking and often we try to run away, to flee from the arena of our annihilation.

One friend had a dream in which three hobos broke into her apartment.[6] Terrified, she called the police, but before they came the men left, leaving her with three gifts. This dream left her with a tremendous feeling of fear, and she didn't realize till later that the three hobos were actually the Magi coming to welcome the newborn Christ. Her fear, like the evil sensed by the couple in the dream, is the reaction of the ego to the destiny of the Self, to the ruthless drive for Truth in which the seeker is sacrificed.

The wine that drugs both the Arab and the couple in the dream is the taste of Unity, awakening the memory of the time when we were one with God and there was no separation. This is the wine that was fermented "before the creation of the vine." It is the blood of the heart, the substance of love that is both intoxicating and addictive. The merest sip of this wine puts the traveller on the path of no return, for its like cannot be found in the world. Its intoxicating nature points beyond the world of the mind, and like a drunkard one is happy to sell everything for just another sip.

This wine belongs to the Beloved, and is given to

those whom He wishes to entice back to a state of unity:

> Verily, Almighty God has a wine for His friends, such that when they drink of it, they become intoxicated, and once they are intoxicated they become merry, and once they are merry, they become purged, and once they are purged they become melted down, and once they are melted down, they become purified, and once they become purified they arrive, and once they arrive they become united with the Divine, and once they are united with the Divine there is no distinction between them and their Beloved.[7]

This wine seduces the wayfarer away from the world of separation, towards the unity that necessitates annihilation. Unity demands the death of the ego. Everything must go, for "when Truth has taken hold of a heart She empties it of all but Herself."[8] In the story of the Arab in Persia, 'Attâr comments that for the secrets of love you must sacrifice everything: "You will lose what you considered to be valuable."[9] The couple in the dream are faced with the same truth which is that they are to be killed. Their sacrifice is the real wine of intoxication.

What is sacrifice and death for the ego is unity and freedom for the soul. This is the harsh truth of the spiritual path and it is also the terrifying bliss of His love. He demands that we belong only to Him.

The couple in the dream were right to be frightened, and the dreamer was warned of the danger of being in the company of lovers. It took her a year to tell this dream, which was greeted only with the comment that Sufis are dangerous people and it is best to stay away. They have nothing to offer, only the tremendous loneliness of longing and the hope of annihilation. But such a group can awaken in a seeker something within the heart that is terrifying to the mind: the taste of Truth.

BEING TOGETHER IN REMEMBRANCE

Remembrance makes people desire the journey:
it makes them into travellers.
Rûmî[1]

TRUTH IS A PAINFUL POISON

Truth is a painful drug because it destroys the illusions with which we protect ourselves. It shatters the barriers of conditioning that confine us within comfortable limitations and it exposes us to a reality that is both unexpected and dangerous. Like the Arab after his encounter with the Qalanders we can be left stunned and poverty stricken, with all our values turned upside down.

A friend once told me a moving story of how her confrontation with Truth left her inwardly shaken for years. She was married when she was eighteen, and her husband was in the army. They both wanted to go to England to visit a spiritual teacher, and very naively did not realize that you cannot just "walk out" of the army. They travelled to Europe and in Germany her husband was arrested by the military police for desertion. She suddenly found herself alone in an unknown land with her husband in prison. All she wanted was to be with him. She had recently read a book which described how in meditation you can leave your body. She practiced the meditation technique described in the book, hoping to leave her body and travel on the astral plane to be with her husband in jail. Such was her longing and desperation that she went into a very deep state of meditation. But she didn't journey to her husband. Instead she experienced the void that underlies creation.

This newly married eighteen-year-old had grown up in ordinary urban America where the physical world is regarded as the only reality, and suddenly she found herself in a deeper dimension in which she experienced the nothingness that is the true inner reality. She experienced that the outer world is just an illusion and that everything she had been brought up to believe in was fundamentally unreal and all the values she had been given were a lie. This was a shattering experience for which her consciousness was unprepared. It terrified her and she felt tremendously alone.

It took her many years to slowly adjust to living in a world which she knew to be an illusion. Luckily she was able to spend some time with a teacher whose presence reassured her that she was not insane. But that experience never left her, for she had tasted the substance of truth that carries the stamp of the beyond. She told me that she spent a lot of time working in her garden, because nature gave her peace. Nature does not deny the inner reality but silently speaks of a state of unity. Nature is not caught in the contradictions of consciousness.

Slowly this woman began to integrate her experience, yet during this time she often felt a stranger amidst those who believed in the reality of what they saw and touched. Silently she carried her secret, sensibly only sharing it with those with whom she felt an inner sympathy. It is a dangerous truth to know that neither you nor the world exist.

In his allegory of the cave,[2] Plato describes how ordinary people live as if in an underground chamber, where they are chained so that they cannot move and can only look at the wall in front of them. On this wall a continual succession of shadows moves, thrown by the light of a fire behind the prisoners. This movement of shadows they take for reality, and what they consider important is how well one is able to remember the sequence of the shadows passing by, and to guess how the shadows may reappear.

One person manages to free himself from his chains and sees that the shadows are not real, only thrown by the firelight. Then he walks up to the entrance of the cave and after a lifetime in the darkness of the cave is dazzled by the sunlight outside. At first the sunlight is so bright he can only see it reflected on the water, but finally he gets used to the real world outside of the cave. He feels sorrow for the people trapped in the cave, who do not even know of the existence of sunlight.

But when he goes back into the cave and sits in his old seat he is blinded by the darkness. He is seen as a fool by those who are still chained watching the shadows on the wall. They say that his visit to the upper world has ruined his vision, and that he has lost sight of what is important: the movement of the shadows.

Truth presents us with a reality so different from that of the sensible world that there can be no comparison. As Dhû-l-Nûn remarked, "Whatever you imagine, God is the opposite of that."[3] How can you compare sunlight to shadows reflected on a wall? And having seen that sunlight, even just for a blinding moment, how can you believe in the progression of shadows? Truth exacts a painful price. If you speak it you are regarded as a fool. Even if you remain silent, you can no longer wholeheartedly join in with the play of illusions that motivates most people on their journey through life.

It is not wise to embark on a quest for Truth. It is dangerous and foolish. A friend had a dream in which she was told this as a simple story about a man lying in bed asleep. At dawn the sunlight came through the window and awoke him. However, the story's narrator said that a wise man would wake before dawn and close the curtains so that he could go back to sleep and not be awakened by the sunlight.

THE TIMELESS MOMENT

In meditation we learn to still the mind and senses and go into the emptiness where Truth is waiting. We willingly enter the nothingness and welcome the dissolution of the ego and all its value structures. In so doing we plant the seeds of our own destruction, because it is the energy of the beyond that annihilates what we think of as ourself. We become the fools of love's call to "open your hidden eyes and come, return to the root of the root of your own self."[4]

When we practice meditation as a group we collectively create a space in which the beyond is made welcome. With the craziness of lovers we collectively throw back the curtains to make sure that we will be awakened by the heart's sunrise. We long for this awakening because we have grown tired of living in a world that is bound by limitation. We seek the horizons of consciousness because we sense what is waiting for us. Collectively we challenge the value systems of the outer world and affirm the infinite dimensions of the heart.

What for the world is a foolish waste of time we affirm in our own individual offering of ourself. Through group meditation the solitary journey of the soul is celebrated in silence. Sitting with friends, when I come out of meditation I am often startled to see that I am in a room full of people. Inwardly there is endless space which honors our real nature. This empty space does not deny our individuality, but embraces what we have to offer: the gift of ourself. Together, as a group, we enter this space in which we are alone. Together we walk the loneliest of paths from the shadows of Plato's cave up to the entrance and the dazzling reality that awaits us. Through a shared sense of purpose we help each other to remember the sunlight that the world has forgotten.

The quality of remembrance is central to the Sufi path. In its essence this remembrance is not just an act of mental recall, bringing something into consciousness from the storehouse of the mind. Rather it is in itself an awakening of an inner awareness of when we united with Him for whom we now search. We long to be with Him because we carry within our heart the memory of this state of oneness. The memory of the heart is distinct from the memory of the mind because the memory of the heart does not belong to time. The mind belongs to time while the heart belongs to eternity. This is why in those moments when we are in love we feel that the love will last forever. Essentially this romantic notion is true. While a month or a year later the love may have dissolved, in the moment we experience it, it is forever because love belongs to the infinite, eternal dimension of the soul. Mother Teresa expresses this truth with simple wisdom:

Small things with great love. It is not how much we do, but how much love we put into doing it. And it is not how much we give, but how much love we put in the giving. To God there is nothing small. The moment we have given it to God it becomes infinite.[5]

Love does not belong to the mind or to the ego. It is part of the deeper mystery of life which links the creation to the Creator. The memories of the heart are memories of love which carry the stamp of our eternal nature. In the core of the heart, what the Sufis refer to as the "heart of hearts," is imprinted the primal memory of love, the memory of being together with God. This is the essential memory which the soul brings into incarnation, and it is the activation of this memory that makes the human being turn away from the world and begin the long journey home.

When the memory of our pre-eternal union with God stirs in the unconscious we begin to feel discontented with the outer world and long to return to the Beloved. The potency of this memory comes from the fact that it does not belong to time. Unlike other memories it does not come from the past but from the eternal present. It offers a direct connection to the dimension of the Self, to that part of our innermost being that is never separate from God.

Remembrance is a dynamic state in which our ordinary consciousness becomes aligned with the inner consciousness of the Self. As we progress along the path this sense of remembrance becomes stronger; our "outer" consciousness is permeated more and more with the quality of our inner state of union and the love that belongs to this oneness. The hidden secret of the heart, which is that in our essence we are never separate from God, becomes more and more a part of our daily life. Whatever our outer circumstances we are contained and nourished by our inner remembrance.

Although remembrance is the essence of the individual journey, it is also present within a group. In a group of sincere seekers there is not only a shared sense of purpose but also a collective memory of being together with God. In the Sufi tradition this timeless moment is referred to as the Primordial Covenant, when God asked the not-yet-created humanity, "Am I not your Lord?" to which we responded, "Yes, we witness it."[6] This "Yes" is the affirmation of our bond with the Beloved, our recognition of His oneness, which we bring into the world of time through our conscious commitment to the path. When a group has as its core this unspoken commitment, this desire to witness Him within the heart, it evokes the heart's remembrance.

We were together with Him before the creation, and in our meditating together with friends that moment is made present. This remembrance can be experienced as a particular quality of silence or intimacy. It can be experienced as both nearness and emptiness, or a strange familiarity. The heart feels at home and sings the song of unity.

It is in this deepest sense that sometimes when people come to a group they feel that they are coming home. Irina Tweedie describes this feeling when she arrived at the railway station of the town where she was to find her teacher:

> Coming home ... my heart was singing. This feeling of joy seized me as soon as I left the train.... It was just one more Indian city, such as

> I had seen many a time before ... and still this
> glorious feeling of coming home, there was no
> earthly reason for it ... it seemed crazy.... The
> fact that I was tired and felt very hot were
> details—for I was coming home.[7]

Instinctively the heart opens and the imprinted memory
becomes alive. In this instant we are as we were before
we were, tasting the wine that we drank before the
creation of the vine. Rûmî celebrates this when he
writes:

> Come out from the circle of time
> And into the circle of love
>
> Enter the street of taverns
> And sit among the drunkards ...
>
> taste a sweetness in your mouth
> that was before honey or bee
>
> look here's a bargain;
> give one life and take a hundred![8]

Entering the street of the taverns, sitting amongst
the friends of God, we find the thread of remembrance,
the golden thread that has always been hidden within
our dreams. But it is wise to be aware of the warning
that this lane of love is a dead-end street—there is no
way out.

SURRENDER AND SIMPLICITY

When we give ourself to Him, we create a space in which He can be present. The greater the surrender the greater the space. There are friends of God who gave themselves to Him long ago and are bound together in love. Individually and as a group they carry the primordial "Yes" as an inner necessity, an instinctual drive to witness His unity. In response to the cry of their hearts He shares the deepest secrets of His oneness:

> the third and highest degree of *tawhîd* [the Unity of God] is the one that God has chosen for Himself, the one of which He alone is worthy; and He radiates from it a ray of light in the consciousness of a group of His chosen ones, while causing them to be silent about defining it and helpless to transmit it....[9]

In their hearts He remembers Himself. He pierces the veils of illusion with His knowledge of His own oneness. His servants carry this knowledge as a lamp which burns them, as a fire which consumes them. This is the pledge they made to Him. This is their work in the world.

The taste of His oneness is intoxicating, but it leaves the victim helplessly burning in the pain of separation. To be amongst the friends of God is to allow oneself to become a casualty of love, to become a drunkard longing only for the next sip of His wine.

The taste of His wine can make the world an empty place, for we have been given a glimpse of something else. We can run away. We can hide. We can believe the doubts and arguments with which our mind will bombard us. Or we can open our hearts and learn to surrender so that He can reveal that *"He is with you ... closer to you than yourself to yourself."*[10]

The mind leads us into complexities, and easily creates an endless succession of problems to occupy our attention. We have become a society of problem solvers. We focus on our problems and are thus confronted with them at every turn, each problem that we solve only evolving into a new problem. Inner truth belongs to the simplicity of the soul. It is not a problem but a presence.

A friend dreamt that she flew to heaven. There in heaven she met God. In her dream God was a Russian foot-soldier, but also very much God. She walked together with God in heaven, which appeared as an industrial landscape. She thought that she should make the most use of this opportunity of being with God, so she asked Him about the problems of the world. He replied that there were no problems. They continued to walk together until she finally said, "I can't believe that you are God." He replied, "That is the only problem."

God, the Ultimate Reality, is unknowable and cannot be named. The Sufi says, "None knows God but God." He is the dazzling darkness in which the lover dissolves and ceases to exist. God in this dream, imaged as a Russian foot-soldier, is more of a personal God, "our Father in heaven," to whom the dreamer can relate and ask questions. One's personal God is one's Higher Self, and spiritual life is learning to be guided by this inner divinity which is our own essence.

For the dreamer the Russian foot-soldier symbol-ized someone very ordinary, and this presented her with the only problem: that someone so ordinary was God. The simplicity of Truth is often bewildering, especially in a culture which has come to value complexity. Yet because the journey to God is a journey from multiplicity back to unity, it will be a journey from the many to the one, from the complexities we experience in the outer world to the simplicity of our own essence. There is a *hadîth,* "God is simple and loves simplicity."[11] But our Western conditioning ill prepares us for the simplicity and ordinariness of our own eternal nature.

In imaging God as a foot-soldier the dreamer's psyche depicts the Self as not only ordinary but also duty-bound. The ego values self-determination and aspires towards the illusory notion of freedom embodied in "doing what you want." Spiritual values are totally opposite: we aspire towards surrender, to being a "yes man" to God. This dream images the esoteric truth that the Higher Self is essentially in a state of surrender, duty-bound to do His will. When we identify with our Higher Self we identify with this innermost state of surrender. We become His servants, and one of His favorite titles is "the servant of His servants."

Learning to surrender to God we are able to embody the Self, to bring the inner surrender of the soul into manifestation. This is why the attitude of surrender is so important, because it aligns our ordinary consciousness with the higher consciousness of the Self. The Self is surrendered to God, and through our attitude of surrender the oneness that is the stamp of the Self is able to come into consciousness; His light is able to shine in our life. Meister Eckhart describes this process of alignment:

> A perfect and true will is one completely
> aligned with God's will and void of everything
> else. The more a man succeeds in following
> God's will, the more he joins in union with God.
> So if someone wishes to touch him, he would
> first have to touch God; if someone wanted to
> approach him, he would first have to pass
> through God. By aligning itself with God's will,
> the soul takes on the taste of God: grief and joy,
> bitterness and sweetness, darkness and light—
> all become divine, whatever happens to this
> man.[12]

In the timeless moment when we agreed to witness
Him, we gave ourself in surrender and tasted the
sweetness of that wine. When that moment is awakened we taste again the essence of surrender and are
seduced into giving ourself back to Him.

But then the mind and the ego step between us
and this eternal moment. We return to the harsh world
of duality and the sweetness remains just as a memory—
yet a memory that drives our instinctual longing to give
ourself to Him. We long to give ourself to Him because
we are already pledged—He calls back those who
belong to Him.

At the beginning we often project onto another
this state of surrender which we long for.[13] It can be too
frightening to acknowledge that we belong so abso-
lutely to Him. Here a teacher figure can help and
inspire us, holding before us the image of our own
surrender. In the following dream the state of surrender is clothed with the awe-inspiring dignity of spiritual poverty:

Together with a few friends I was sitting in my teacher's kitchen. She was sitting on a wooden chair in the corner. Opposite her was a door through which could be seen a larger room full of people in meditation. Amongst us in the kitchen there was a feeling of expectancy as if we were waiting for the teacher to say something special. She got up as if she was going to make this announcement and I realized that she was wearing old clothes, an old black sweater, and her stockings had rolled down to her slippers. Although she was wearing these old clothes there was an awe-inspiring feeling of dignity about her.

Her head was turned upwards but her eyes were closed, and I realized that this awe-inspiring quality of dignity came from the fact that somewhere she was so utterly surrendered that she would not do or say anything without the direct will of God. As I realized this she opened her mouth as if she was about to say something, and then she hesitated and stopped and didn't speak. I knew that despite the pressure of the people waiting for her to say something, as far as she was concerned she was not going to say anything without its being His will.

When he told the dream, the dreamer said that something within his heart stood to attention as he experienced this inner happening. He experienced a state of inner obedience that is total and absolute. His heart responded with the lover's desire to stand before God and await His command.

Through the dream the Self brings its nature into consciousness. It connects the dreamer with the innermost state of surrender that is His imprint. Then the dreamer needs to accept and learn to live this surrender, to become a "yes man," duty-bound to enact His will. This may seem too frightening, too absolute, too demanding. We can run away, hide from the call of the Self, accept the ego's demands for self-determination and its fantasies of freedom. But deep within the heart we know that real freedom is bought with sacrifice, and only through the total sacrifice of ourself can we be released into the freedom of slavery.

In this dream the teacher wears old clothes and yet has an awe-inspiring quality of dignity. This dignity comes from the fact that she will do nothing unless it is His will. It is a quality of the nobility of the Self, a nobility that manifests through a state of spiritual poverty in which one is dependent only upon God because one has given oneself to Him. It is symbolized by the color black which is no color. In this state the mystic is "so totally absorbed in God that he has no longer any existence of his own, neither inwardly nor outwardly in this world and beyond; he returns to his original essential poverty, and that is poverty in the true sense."[14] We return to "what we were before we were," to the state of surrender at the eternal moment when we affirmed that He is our Lord.

Sufis bow down only before God. We belong to Him because we gave ourself to Him before the beginning. The journey home takes us back to this moment which is eternally present. Slowly we uncover the true nature of our relationship with Him, which is waiting within us. We return to:

A condition of complete simplicity
(Costing not less than everything).[15]

WALKING THROUGH THE DOORWAY
OF THE DREAM

The relationship with God is the relationship with our own inner essence. It is a process of returning from the many to the one, to the state of inner unity that we carry as a seed within us. Sitting together with friends we place this seed into the emptiness where He is present. The group remembrance affirms our own remembrance. In this space of togetherness His unity germinates this seed and protects it from the complex patterns of the mind and problems that belong to the ego. It is only His presence, the energy of His consciousness, that enables the whole process of inner awakening to take place: only "in thy light shall we see light."[16]

Through dreams, visions, and glimpses in meditation we are allowed to know a little about this tremendous mystery that is taking place within us. In telling our dreams, sharing our visions, we bring this mystery into the outer world where it can nourish our ordinary everyday life. Sadly, we often experience the outer world as a hostile environment, antagonistic to the inner journey. There, surrender is seen only as a weakness and the idea of poverty is incompatible with dignity. A group is so important because it provides a safe haven, a place in the outer world where the values of the inner world are held precious. Weary travellers find a safety they have not known in their outer life. Lovers and drunkards find that their longing for intoxication is not despised but encouraged by the silent presence of remembrance. Slowly the secrets of the heart are able to yield up their fragrance, and so we help each other. Telling our travellers' tales and lovesick stories we welcome the unknowable, and in turn feel the welcome that only the unknowable can give.

A group can provide a container to help us realize our longings, help make our deepest dreams a living reality. But we are always thrown back upon ourself, back into the depths where our treasure is hidden. The sense of security that the group provides is a stepping stone to the real security of the heart. Our dreams image an inner dynamic and the group helps us to understand and integrate these messages. But in the end these are only pointers on a path which we have to walk alone. We have to confront the monsters, the threatening figures that come out from the shadows, and we have to claim and honor the beauty and radiance that is revealed.

Our dreams open a doorway into the inner world, but it is for us to step through, to participate as fully as we can in our own mystery. We need to feel this inner world and allow its pain and wonder, its despair and longing, into consciousness. We need to take the substance of our dream and make it real through inner attention, allowing ourself to be often bewildered and confused in the process. Vulnerable and foolish we stand like Parsifal before the Holy Grail, and we must ask the question, commit ourself to the miracle. Otherwise the dream remains just as a possibility, a story of something that might have been....

Our dreams lead us deeper and deeper, luring us into the unknown. Finally they leave us standing on the edge of the abyss and we know then that there is nowhere to go. The journey has ended and we have arrived nowhere. Then there is no group and no support, and sitting amidst friends we feel only desolation. In the unbearable emptiness we are left alone to die, not knowing that in this moment the journey is over because we have been found.

A journey implies movement and progression. We search for Him with every effort until, weary and exhausted, we give up. We have to look, even though the object of our search never left us, but is with us in our looking:

> I will search for the Friend with all my passion
> and all my energy, until I learn
> that I don't need to search....
>
> But that knowing depends
> on the time spent looking.[17]

Driven by the instinct that somewhere He has to be found, we walk in the dust and heat of the road, chased by dogs and laughed at by villagers who are sensible enough to stay at home. But of course there is nowhere to go, because He for whom we search is not separate from us. Our search leads us to the place of desperation until finally our heart breaks open to the emptiness where He is always present, to the timeless moment of love in which we are bonded together.

We need to search in order to find what was always within us, because only then do we know our real nature. Sufis tell a story about some fishes who made the great journey in order to find out what water is:

> There was a lake and in this lake there lived many fish. It was a beautiful lake. There was enough to eat, there were many trees around the lake. The sun shone almost every day because

it was in the south. The water was not too cold and the fish were very, very happy. But one day after a heavy rain in the hills, the river swelled and carried into the lake a trout.

"Ha," said the trout, "this is a lake and bigger than the river. But this lake is really a boring place."

So the trout swam around and looked at everything, and said, "Water is not flowing here. There is nothing that interests me to eat here. I want flies and there are no flies here. There are just a lot of silly little fish." And the trout jumped into the air and said, "I bet they don't even know what water is," and he swam back into the river.

The fish looked at each other and said, "What did he say? We don't know what water is? I wonder what he can mean!" And so they founded a university and had workshops and seminars and intellectual exercises, and invited wise fish. However, nobody was able to tell them what water is. So little by little they became depressed, and had conflicts and needed psychological healing. But none of it helped. Then one day someone remembered that far, far away, at the end of the seventh lake, there was a very wise fish. He was hundreds of years old. He was so mighty and wonderful that he was all silver. So they decided to swim there and ask him what water is.

They swam through the first lake, where some were caught by eagles and others by fishermen. In the second lake more were caught, and others became too tired to go on while still others found tasty morsels and were diverted from the journey. So it went on until out of the hundreds who had started only thirty or forty arrived in the seventh lake. At the end of that lake there was a cave, and in that cave there was a very big, silver fish. It was enormous and almost blind, and it was in *samadhi*. The little fishes all made a circle around him and waited.

Eventually the wise old fish opened his eyes, which twinkled, looked around him and said, "Brothers, why have you come here? What do you want?"

"Sir," one of them timidly said, "we came to ask you a question."

"What is the question?" asked the wise old fish.

"Sir, we want to know what is water."

The wise old fish did not answer, but he closed his eyes and went back into *samadhi*. The little fish stayed there, patiently but with pumping hearts.

After a long while he opened his eyes, and said, "My friends, I do not know what water is. But I can tell you what water is not. Water is not the sky, water is not the clouds, it is not the grass, it is not the stones, it is not the trees." And he talked for a very long time telling them what water is not. Then he closed his eyes and went back into *samadhi*.

So the fish looked at each other and said, "He told us what water is not. Ah! Maybe water is where we are!"

And they became very happy, and swam away back to their little lake and lived happily ever after.

TURNED ON THE POTTER'S
WHEEL

Now the Lord is with them in every alteration,
Performing an unimaginable work in them hour after hour.
If they only knew *they would not withdraw from Him*
even for the space of a wink.
For He does not withdraw from them at any time.
Al-Hallâj[1]

TRANSFORMATION BEYOND THE SELF

One of the greatest mysteries of the path is that we are
remade, inwardly transformed in a manner that is far
beyond our comprehension. He is the greatest artist,
and the whole miracle of creation is a testimony to His
creative powers. Each leaf on the tree, each flower
opening to the sun, has a simplicity and beauty that are
a wonder. Human beings are the pinnacle of creation,
and are themselves consciously able to create, to make
both beauty and horror out of His gift of consciousness. But when a human being gives himself back to
the Creator, consciously offers himself on the altar of
love and devotion, the Beloved performs His greatest
miracle: the inner transformation of a human being.

The notion of "self-transformation" has become
part of the "new age" culture, yet our Western ego-
oriented conditioning can make it difficult for us to

accept that we are not the agents of transformation. The ego will not take us beyond the ego, as in the old song, "you can't get to heaven in a rocking chair, 'cause a rocking chair won't rock that far."

We have to confront our fear of surrendering to something beyond our control and beyond our understanding. But we also have to contend with a collective conditioning that asserts the supremacy of the mind and the ego and does not acknowledge a transcendent dynamic. The very idea that on the inner journey we know neither where to go nor how to get there threatens a consciousness which is educated and conditioned to plan and be in control. This is poignantly illustrated by the continual mistranslation of the saying of the Greek philosopher Heraclitus. Speaking of the search for Truth, Heraclitus writes: "Unless you expect the unexpected you will never find because it is undiscoverable and pathless." Yet Western academics are so threatened by the implications of this direct and yet paradoxical statement that the text has been blatantly mistranslated into an acceptable form: "Unless you expect the unexpected, you'll never find, because it is hard to find and difficult to discover."

The pathless nature of this journey for Truth is so threatening to the mind and the ego because it involves surrender. We have to give ourself to Him in order that He can take us Home, as is simply stated in a Sufi poem:

> No one by himself
>   can find the path to Him
> Whoever goes to His street
>   goes with His feet.[2]

The wayfarer does not transform himself; rather he is transformed. Soon after a friend came to our group he had the following dream which outlined both his intention to create something and the real process in which he would be remade:

> I was seated at a potter's wheel
> Unmolded clay in my hands
> And the wheel was turning ...
> My intent, I believe, was to mold a simple cup ...
>
> But I knew nothing of molding clay
> And as the wheel turned,
> The clay itself would not take shape
> And the constant turning forced it
> Into unnatural shapes now bending
> One way, then the other ...
> In all ways out of my control.
>
> And then a man's hand appeared
> And placed his palm and fingers over mine.
> The hand became an arm,
> Became a man's full form
> Enfolding my despair ...
> And with a gentleness in strength,
> Guided me in the molding
> As a father would a child.
>
> And as we together moved
> In the turning task,
> I let his way be mine
> And I became the clay ...
> Thus centered on the potter's wheel

My body flowed into a new cup rising
Open to receive ...
A chalice of emptiness
Which my Beloved has molded out of me.

This dream spoke with the wisdom of the Self, outlining for the dreamer the whole process of inner transformation. The dream leads him from his initial intention to "mold a cup," to create something which could be of service, to himself being a "chalice of emptiness." At the beginning he does not know how to work with clay and only forces the clay into unnatural shapes. How often, with the best of intentions, do we try to transform ourselves, only creating further problems and difficulties.

THE ATTITUDE NECESSARY FOR INNER WORK

The basic premise for all inner work is that we do not know what to do. We do not know how to transform ourselves, and this inner process cannot be forced. One of the dangers of the present time is that many psychological and spiritual techniques offering self-transformation are easily available. Often with the best of intentions we try them, not realizing how delicate is the structure of the human psyche and how careful we have to be with all inner work. Between our conscious and unconscious self there is a filter that enables us to live without being overwhelmed by the contents of the psyche. We can have access to the nourishment of the inner world through dreams, intuition, and creative work, and yet at the same time live a balanced outer life. But once we start tampering with the filter system, upsetting the balance of consciousness and the unconscious, we can only too easily end up very disturbed, in the worst cases flooded by the endless ocean of the psyche.

Psychological techniques can easily open us to the unconscious, but it may not be so easy to close this door. Jung was very aware of the dangers of working with the images of the unconscious and the attitude of responsibility this work requires:

> The images of the unconscious place a great responsibility upon a man. Failure to understand them, or a shirking of ethical responsibility, deprives him of his wholeness and imposes a painful fragmentation upon his life.[3]

For example, someone who came to our group dreamed that there were two cages full of birds, and the birds were drinking water from a barrel and then falling down dead. Such a dream not only needs to be understood, it also places a certain responsibility upon the dreamer. The dreamer recognized the birds as images of her aspirations and intuitions, and wondered why they were not free, and worse still, why were they dying? Surely such birds should drink from the living waters of life and not from some stagnant barrel? In fact the dream prompted her to change her relationship with these inner birds. She was able to free her aspirations from a certain rigid, conditioned outlook on life, which the dream had allowed her to recognize.

But if one does not take such a dream seriously then a certain regression takes place as part of one's consciousness becomes trapped in the unconscious. Once the door to the inner world is opened, if one does not take a responsible attitude and consciously reflect upon what the unconscious is trying to communicate, then the unconscious becomes negative. Facing the Gorgon's head without Perseus's shield of conscious reflection, one is turned to stone; part of oneself is swallowed by the Great Mother. Psychological window-shopping is a dangerous business.

Once a woman asked me about the possible reasons for her not remembering her dreams. I replied that maybe she did not need to dream. Some people are so in tune with their unconscious that there is no need for the unconscious to communicate through the medium of dreams. For example, some artists and musicians express their inner self through their art, and thus have no need to dream. A friend of mine who composes music very rarely dreams. Her access to her inner self is through her music, and it is in music that her unconscious expresses itself. However, the woman who asked about not remembering her dreams felt that this did not apply to her. So I suggested that possibly she repressed her dreams because she did not really want to know what was in her unconscious. At first she asserted that she did want to get in touch with her unconscious. I asked her if she was really prepared to take responsibility for what she found within herself, and to put in the years of hard work, years of confronting painful and unpleasant aspects of herself, that it might take to integrate what her dreams might reveal. She was honest enough to say that she did not want to do this work. Such honesty is far better than entering into the inner world without an attitude of responsibility.

Spiritual techniques pose a similar if not more dangerous threat than psychological work. In the previous chapter I described how an unsuspecting eighteen-year-old was thrown into a reality for which she was totally unprepared. This was just through a simple meditation practice. Other spiritual techniques, particularly breathing practices, can awaken inner energies. This can be exhilarating, but these energies need to be contained; otherwise they can cause both physical and psychological problems. Furthermore, these energies once awakened are not always able to be put back to sleep.

Usually it is the attitude of the individual that is all-important. If we are sincere and intend to help heal the wounds of the inner world, to work in service for the Self, then the Self protects and helps us. But if we are attracted to practice psychological or spiritual techniques out of idle curiosity, or, worse, for the power purposes of the ego, then the results can be damaging. Just as there is greed for material possessions and worldly power, so is there greed for inner experiences or inner power. Human beings are as delicately balanced as the ecosystem, and psychological or spiritual greed can be as destructive to the psyche as material greed has been to the earth.

Many fairy tales image the danger of entering the inner world for personal greed. The stepdaughter who greets the gnomes with kindness is rewarded with magical gifts, while her half-sister who seeks these figures for greed receives only a curse. The same dynamic is portrayed in this African story:

> In an African village a group of young women banded together to humiliate one girl of whom they were jealous, particularly because she had a more beautiful bead necklace than any of them. So, one day, when they were all beside the river, they hid their necklaces and then told

her that they had thrown their necklaces into the river as an offering to the river god. She should do likewise.

The kindhearted girl took off her necklace and threw it into the river, whereupon the other girls retrieved their necklaces from where they had been hidden, and ran off laughing. The young girl was left forlorn and sad. She wandered along the river bank praying to the river god to help restore her necklace. Then she heard a voice telling her to jump into a nearby pool. Without hesitation she jumped in, and found herself on the river bed, where an old woman sat waiting. This woman, who was ugly and covered in open sores, said to the girl, "Lick my sores." The kind girl did as she was asked, and licked the repulsive sores, whereupon the old woman said, "Because you have been so compassionate, I will hide and protect you when the demon comes who devours the flesh of young women." At that moment there was a great roar and a terrible monster appeared, saying that he smelt a maiden there. But the old woman had hidden the girl, so he went away cursing.

Then the old crone said to the girl, "Here is your necklace," and she handed her a necklace many times more beautiful than the one which had been lost. The girl thanked her for it and then found herself on the river bank. She returned to her village, and meeting the other girls, astonished them with the beauty of her new necklace. They asked her where she had gotten it, and she said that it had been given to her by an old woman in the river.

The girls of the village were even more jealous, and without more ado rushed off to the river, threw their own necklaces in, and jumped in after them. At the bottom of the river they met the old woman, who once again said, "Lick my sores." But these girls just laughed at her and said that they wouldn't dream of doing anything so repulsive, and asked her for their new necklaces. At that moment the demon appeared and devoured them all.[4]

A necklace is an ancient symbol for a woman's identity. This story describes how the collective, the young women, can deny one's individuality. The journey to retrieve the necklace takes the kindhearted girl into the waters of the unconscious, where she meets the crone, an aspect of her feminine self. The crone is covered in repulsive sores because this aspect of feminine wisdom, which is neither virgin nor mother, has been rejected and carries the pain of the shadow. The inner journey involves working to heal the wounds in the unconscious, a painful task in which one has to confront, accept, and love these wounds.

The young girl gives herself unconditionally to this shadow work and her attitude protects her from the monster, the devouring aspect of the unconscious. The crone rewards her with a necklace "many times more beautiful than the one that had been lost," for it is in the unconscious, hidden behind the shadow, that one finds the beauty of one's real nature, the unique work of the Greatest Artist. However, the story warns of the dangers of entering the unconscious without a similar commitment to inner work—the selfish village girls are devoured.

Entering the unconscious means confronting the pain of the shadow. The shadow stands like a guardian of the treasures of the inner world. It is the *prima materia*, the basic substance of our own transformation and at the same time the testing ground of the attitude we bring to our quest. If we take our inner work seriously and are prepared to accept the pain of our rejected self, then we will be welcomed and helped. But it is best to stay away from any inner work, from any psychological or spiritual techniques, if we are not willing to take responsibility for what we find in the depths.

THE POINT OF DESPAIR

When we enter into the inner world we need to be conscious and to take responsibility for what we may find in the depths. Yet at the same time, paradoxically, we need to surrender to the unknown. For it is only when we give ourself into the arms of our invisible Beloved that our heart opens to the infinite and the real work of transformation takes place. The consciousness and attitude of responsibility required for this work have nothing at all to do with controlling or shaping our experience, but rather with a commitment to face and accept whatever we come upon. In fact it is often through a recognition of our inability to control or shape events that we learn the surrender necessary for this work.

In the dream of the potter's wheel the dreamer tries to mold his own cup, but he fails; he knows nothing of the process and the clay is always out of his control. Yet the despair which he feels is the prelude to surrender. We despair because we realize that alone we cannot find the treasure that we long for; we cannot by ourselves answer the soul's deepest longing. Yet if we allow the feeling of despair to permeate our whole being, the intensity of this feeling pushes aside the ego and allows us to surrender. Our inner need cries from the depths of the heart and fills us with emptiness and longing. Only He can satisfy this need and as a lover He responds. The dreamer feels the gentle strength of Another "enfolding my despair." From then on the dreamer is guided in the process of molding his own chalice.

In despair we give ourself back to Him. We are confronted with the realization that alone we are helpless and cannot make the journey. We need His guidance, yet He cannot guide us until we step aside. Only one pilot can take the ship of our soul into the eternal waters of the Self. In our despair we surrender our free will, we give back the gift He gave us, and then He reveals His way. The Sufi poet Nazir describes how his search led him to despair. His heart burning with fire he sought his Beloved, and yet was tormented by the awareness that:

> I knew nothing:
>> I knew not what to seek,
>> I knew not where to go.[5]

The poet searches everywhere, in the mosque, in the temple, on pilgrimages, in the wilderness, and in the forest, but nowhere can he find his Beloved: "The Lord would not show Himself to me." Finally he reaches the state of total despair, thinking he can do no more than die.[6] This is the moment of surrender in which the ego "dies," giving space for Him to reveal Himself:

When I reached a state of total despair,
   hoping that death
   might rescue me from this pain,
   He, my careless Beloved,
Came to me.
Like a mother rushing to her sick child,
He came to me,
   sat by my side,
   and placed my head upon His lap.
Kind words flowed from His lips:

"Now see whatever you want to see,
I will reveal to you all the secrets of my heart.
Remember, first we test our lover;
   torture him, oppress him,
   and force him to shed tears.
Then we invite him to us.
When all his thoughts are of the Beloved,
We allow him to come near,
   shower him with grace,
   and hold him in our arms.
Thus he becomes perfect."[7]

In our despair we know that only He can take us to Him. Standing alone and vulnerable we can either retreat in fear or give ourself to the darkness where He is present.

We begin the journey hoping to find something, and are only confronted with our own pain and inadequacy. One friend told me that it had been three years since she had seriously begun her inner search. At the beginning she had experienced two months of bliss and since then she had only known suffering. But what frightened her most was that she had always hoped that she would be transformed, and instead she experienced an endless process in which she was becoming empty of everything, even her hope. Now she felt desperate and alone.

In our despair and aloneness we cry to Him. Transformation is not a process of becoming something but of losing everything so that there is space for Him. Through suffering we are made empty so that He can be present—there is not enough room in the heart for both the ego and the Beloved. Even hope has to go, because it is a hope for something and we have to become nothing. On the potter's wheel we are made into "a chalice of emptiness." Only then are we able to hold the wine of His love for us.

A CHALICE OF EMPTINESS

We search but we cannot find. In our aloneness and despair we give ourself to Him. The ego surrenders and the real process of spiritual transformation begins. In the dream of the potter's wheel the dreamer becomes the clay and not the potter. The clay gives itself to the hands of the real Potter and is turned into "a new cup."

Through the act of surrender the inner alignment of the wayfarer shifts from the ego to the Self. Surrender creates an empty space in which our transcendent center of being can manifest into consciousness. The Self is eternally present but veiled by the desires of the ego. It is for this reason that people with a strong sense of ego cannot live a guided life. They are ruled by the ego, by their desire to determine their own life. In surrendering we do not repress the ego but step aside from its known horizons, from its patterns and preoccupations into a state of vulnerability and unknowing. It is this inner feeling of exposure and helplessness that is so threatening and which can so easily throw us back into the grip of the ego

But if the longing and despair are strong enough we give ourself willingly into the tender and terrifying emptiness. Our inner center shifts from the ego to the Self, from what is fluctuating and transitory to what is eternally present. The Self as a center of consciousness gives us an inner stability that enables the process of spiritual transformation to proceed at a much higher frequency. Through the act of surrender the heart opens and starts to spin us faster and faster, cleansing us of impurities and taking us beyond the mind. If we have not surrendered, this speeding up could throw us wildly off balance. But centered in the Self, we give our whole self unconditionally to the process of being made "featureless and formless,"[8] a chalice of emptiness for the Beloved:

> Thus centered on the potter's wheel
> My body flowed into a new cup rising
> Open to receive...
> A chalice of emptiness
> Which my Beloved has molded out of me.

Searching for Truth we are confronted with our own pain, our own darkness, and the empty nothingness that is the dimension of the Self. The harshness, the bleakness, and the intoxicating nature of this journey cannot be compared to anything we may find in the outer world. Our collective conditioning has created a picture of self-transformation in which we arrive somewhere and become somebody, when in reality we arrive nowhere and become nothing. We can never be prepared for what is unknowable, but we can de-condition ourself, and learn to "expect the unexpected." Our dreams can help to point out the pathless nature of the journey and so inwardly align us with this insane venture. They can counter the collective conditioning, allowing us to be love's fools and search for a Beloved who never left us. When we share these dreams in a group we all benefit from hearing this senseless story; the heart rejoices because it knows we cannot know. In embracing our own inability to know the way, we praise Him who guides us. In the words of Abû Bakr, "Praise to God who hath given His creatures no way of attaining to the knowledge of Him except through their inability to know Him."[9]

Each dream tells of the dreamer's own individual encounter with the beyond. Some dreams point to buried treasure or image roads that lead the dreamer to golden cities. So we begin with the idea of a goal and a journey. But as Rûmî says:

> a journey to the sea
> is horses and fodder and contrivance
> but at land's end
> the footsteps vanish.[10]

The search takes us to the land's end, to the door of the endless ocean of the heart. He waits within, always unknowable, demanding only that we dissolve into Him until no trace is left.

In the following dream the dreamer comes to the open door of her teacher's hut. But within there is only darkness and an ominous wind:

> I go to visit the teacher who lives in a small hut. I open the door. I know that the teacher is at home, yet when I open the door there is no one there, nothing but darkness, a blackness

more absolute than anything I have seen before.
Apart from the darkness, all I am aware of is an
ominous wind. It blows in the house like a wind
of change, and I hear a slight rustle like the
blowing of plastic garbage bags. I stand on the
doorstep and feel afraid.

This dream was given to the dreamer soon after she
came to our group. Like the dream of the potter's wheel
it outlines a process of inner transformation. It is not
what the dreamer expects.

The teacher, being someone surrendered to God,
merged with the Absolute Emptiness, is often a symbol
for the dreamer's Higher Self and spiritual aspirations.
To go to visit a teacher is the beginning of the quest
when we aspire to realize our inner connection with
the Self. Yet the dream points out the terrifying truth:
there is no one there. In the very depths of our being
we are just an endless empty space, without form.
There is "nothing but darkness, a blackness more
absolute than anything I have seen before." This is "the
black light of the *Deus absconditus,* the hidden treasure that aspires to reveal itself."[11] This is the void, the
absolute nothingness of Truth that lies beyond the
mind. It is experienced in the state of *fanâ*, the
annihilation of the ego, in which individual consciousness is totally dissolved in the uncreated dark light of
God. Jâmî describes the absolute nature of this state:

Self-annihilation consists in this, that through
the overpowering influence of the Very Being
upon the inner man, there remains no consciousness of aught besides Him. Annihilation
of annihilation consists in this, that there remains no consciousness even of that uncon-

sciousness. It is evident that annihilation of annihilation is involved in annihilation.[12]

Entering the arena of the Self, symbolized in the dream by the simple hut of the teacher, commences the process of dissolution. If we surrender to this process we will be taken beyond the ego into the nothingness in which the lover and the Beloved are united.

Looking in through the teacher's door the dreamer sees the darkness and feels an ominous wind. This is the wind of the spirit which heralds the birth of the Self:

> The wind bloweth where it listeth, and thou hearest the sound thereof, but canst not tell where it cometh, and whither it goeth: so is every one that is born of the spirit.[13]

The wind of the spirit comes from the beyond and breaks down the patterns and defenses of the ego. It strips the human being of inner and outer attachments until he or she is left naked and defenseless. For the ego this wind is the herald of death. "It blows in the house like a wind of change," and it has an ominous feeling. The dreamer is being warned of the consequences of stepping over the threshold.

The Sufi teacher Bhai Sahib used to refer to his house as "a house of drunkards and a house of change." In the presence of love we lose our senses and we lose our selves. What is death to the ego is bliss to the Higher Self. Empty of our self we are a space in which He can experience Himself, reveal to Himself the mysteries of His own heart, intoxicate Himself with His own nearness.

The wind blows in the darkness. All that seems to

be present in the empty hut are some plastic garbage bags. The dreamer cannot see these bags, but hears them rustle in the wind. Sufis are known as the "sweepers" or "garbage bins of humanity" for we absorb the darkness in people's hearts so that they can come closer to Him.

At the beginning of the journey we are confronted by our own refuse, the rejected parts of our self that we have repressed in the darkness. This refuse is the cornerstone of our own transformation, the secret of our own wholeness. As we work upon the shadow, accepting, loving, and integrating what arises from the unconscious, we find the light of the Self which had been hidden in the depths. Gradually the Self unveils its light, and this unveiling speeds up the process of transformation. In the light of the Self we can see our own self more clearly, and we are given an inner security that enables us to delve into the deepest and most disturbing areas of our personal and collective wounds. The embrace of the Self allows us to be vulnerable and open so that His love can permeate throughout our whole being. It is our openness to His love that determines the degree of our own transformation.

But the work on the shadow is only a preparation for a life of service. The shadow teaches us the lesson of humility. Having experienced the depths of our own darkness we can never judge another person, nor can we be frightened by the darkness. Work on the shadow also gives us the inner stability and strength that we need if we are to work with others. Finally, when our heart has been swept clean He uses it for His own purposes. Sufis are the servants of humanity and through the hearts of His lovers He is able to do His work in the world.

The work on the shadow takes us beyond the darkness of the psyche to the absolute darkness of the unknowable Reality. Then we return to the world, empty and unknowing, to be used as He wills. Standing in her teacher's doorway the dreamer is right to be afraid. This is a journey in which nothing is found and everything is lost. It is a journey from duality back to unity, from individuality to annihilation. We return to the primal unity that was before we experienced separation:

> In God there is no duality. In that Presence "I" and "we" and "you" do not exist. "I" and "you" and "He" become one.... Since in Unity there is no distinction, the Quest and the Way and the Seeker become one.[14]

It is this mystery of His own oneness that He gradually reveals in the heart of His lover. Because He loves us He longs to make real this innermost secret within us. He empties our heart of all traces of duality until it becomes a chalice of emptiness spinning on the wheel of love.

DOORKEEPERS OF LOVE

Be with those who mix with God
as honey blends with milk, and say,
"Anything that comes and goes,
rises and sets, is not
what I love."

Rûmî[1]

HIS PRESENCE AND HIS ABSENCE

The hearts of His lovers are aligned with love. They tasted the wine of union before the creation of the vine: they belong to Him since before the beginning of time. Yet they also know the pain of separation, the wailing song of the reed torn from the reed bed.

"God is the sigh of the soul," for He has created in our hearts the longing for love. Our longing is His longing. In our heart He longs to come closer to Himself. We are the vehicle for His longing and His love. This is the inner truth of every prayer and every aspiration, as al-Hallâj expresses in simple logic:

> I call to you. No it is You who calls me to
> Yourself.
> How could I say "It is You!"—if you had not said
> to me "It is I."[2]

We long for Him because we already know Him. Our longing is the fruit of our pre-eternal state of union.

In the depths of our heart we know Him and are together with Him. Yet our heart also cries with the pain of separation. Thus in our heart we embrace both His presence and His absence. We know the innermost bliss of His nearness and the longing of creation to return to the Creator. We hold in our heart these opposites, and the tremendous tension they create breaks us and transforms us. There is no greater polarity, no greater tension of opposites than His presence and His absence.

That He is present within His creation is one of the greatest revelations. That He appears absent and unknown in His own world lies at the root of all our searching. Ibn 'Arabî expresses the paradox of this mystery:

> God deposited with man knowledge of all things, then prevented him from perceiving what he had deposited within him.... This is one of the divine mysteries which reason denies and considers totally impossible. The nearness of this mystery to those ignorant of it is like God's nearness to His servant, as mentioned in His words, "We are nearer to him than you, but you do not see" (Sura 56:85), and His words, "We are nearer to him than the jugular vein" (Sura 50:16). In spite of this nearness, the person does not perceive and does not know.... No one knows what is within himself until it is unveiled instant by instant.... [3]

As in the story of the little fishes we make the greatest journey to discover the nature of the invisible substance in which we exist. Gradually He reveals the tremendous truth of His presence.

The little fishes were only told what water is not. Then they realized that "water is where we are!" One friend had a similar experience when, sitting in meditation, he saw that he was waiting for a spiritual experience. He realized that this desire belonged to the ego and was really an obstacle. He saw this desire as if in front of him, and then from behind—from the opposite direction of the desire—he experienced the vast nothingness that is the inner reality. Experiencing the limitation of every desire he was able to glimpse behind the veil of the ego and feel the empty presence that is the hidden essence of everything. Seeking what we cannot define, we have to surrender to this wondrous emptiness that underlies creation:

> I saw You and became empty.
> This Emptiness, more beautiful than existence,
> it obliterates existence, and yet when It comes,
> existence thrives and creates more existence!
>
> The sky is blue. The world is a blind man
> squatting on the road.
>
> But whoever sees Your Emptiness
> sees beyond blue and beyond the blind man....
>
> To praise is to praise
> how one surrenders
> to the Emptiness.[4]

THE BORDER OF THE BEYOND

Seeking Him we are led to the border of the beyond, to the place where consciousness meets the vast nothingness. Usually we encounter this primal absence first in meditation, and the mind may recoil in fear. Everything we know, everything we think we are, is lost in this darkness. But gradually we forget our fears. This nothingness is imbued with the invisible energy of love, which holds us as we lose our bearings and ourselves. We learn to give ourselves gladly to the void. We sense the ultimate security it offers and taste the peace which is not of this world.

When we return to the outer world there is sometimes an inhuman light in the eyes, a memory of the beyond which does not belong to the mind. Slowly the ego and the mind return and, taking their place of seeming precedence, try to fill us with their desires and doubts. But inwardly we know that we have tasted something else: we have been lost in the source.

Living our outer life we work in the world, and yet inwardly we become more and more absorbed. We learn to stand on the border of the beyond. We have always held in our heart both His presence and His absence. Now this mystery of the heart becomes a part of our consciousness. We sense the desolation of a world that does not know Him, and we feel how love's formlessness is so infinitely tender. These apparent opposites are molded together in our love for Him. We feel both His separation and His nearness.

Through longing our hearts are made empty and open, and we are receptive to His need to bring love into His world. Unknowingly we become a place in time where love is made manifest. Our heart is love's threshold and our whole being becomes attuned to the energy of love as it flows into the world. It is for this purpose that He shared with us the secret mystery of His aloneness, the timeless moment of His oneness. In the innermost chamber of the heart He aligned us with the central core of love—our heart aligned to His heart. Our surrender is a process of attunement, of bringing this inner alignment of the heart into consciousness. Then the outer and inner worlds can be linked in love and this energy can flow into manifestation through the open door of His lovers' hearts.

Through the spiritual practices of meditation and *dhikr* we give ourselves to the remembrance of the Beloved. Through our effort and will the practice of remembrance becomes more and more constant. The memory of the primordial covenant, when we answered His question, "Am I not your Lord?" with the affirmation, "Yes, we witness it,"[5] becomes alive within the heart. This is the stamp of His remembrance of Himself which gradually permeates our whole being. Outwardly life continues with its everyday difficulties and conflicts. But inwardly He whose name we repeat becomes a living reality of love. This process is portrayed in the following dream experience:

> Was practicing, practicing, practicing. All the time I was practicing the *dhikr* and it was wonderful. Things went on. My husband became irritated with me over some chore. The children quarrelled. My mother even appeared at one point. The most mundane things were all around and it made no difference because something was in me due to the practice. My only thought was to keep practicing.
>
> In the practice no words were said or thought. It is something not quite said or thought, but a

golden livingness inside. Cannot truly express
what it was—but wonderful past descriptions. It
was not just a *dhikr*—it was alive. And I say, "I
was practicing" because my will was needed for
it to go on. It required my will at every moment
to go on—but otherwise nothing was done by
me.

Al-Ghazzâlî wrote that "*Dhikr* is, in its reality, the pro-
gressive power of the Named on the heart, while the
dhikr itself wears away and disappears." Through our
remembrance He opens us to the eternal moment of
His presence.

Sufis are doorkeepers of love. Our heart is opened
so that His love can come into the world. Our heart is
made to spin with the vibration of His love for
humanity. The more we give ourself to Him, the more
we are inwardly absorbed into the emptiness, the
larger the doorway of the heart.

Working in the world, living our everyday life, we
are a space for His love to flow where He wills.
Sometimes the lover feels how his heart is used to
touch another's heart, but mostly we are unaware of
how the Beloved uses us. The less the ego knows about
the deepest purposes of the heart the less there is the
possibility for inflation or pride. We try to remain free
from any identification; our attention should remain
focused on the Beloved.

Sufis work this way not only individually but also
in groups. Any group which meditates together brings
light into the world. A spiritual group is a point of light
in space which has a beneficial influence upon its
surroundings. This light helps to create harmony. It can
awaken individuals to their own inner call, help them
to see more clearly their own light. This effect does not

depend upon any conscious connection with the particular meditation group, as is illustrated by the experience of John who lived for a number of years next door to a Sufi group. When John moved into the next-door apartment he was a stockbroker and a new BMW was parked outside. In the next year or so the stock market flourished and soon a Porsche was parked beside the BMW. Then suddenly one day both the BMW and the Porsche disappeared and instead there was a small rental car. John had left the stock market and was going to Canada for a year to train as a yoga teacher. A year later he returned to sell his apartment and moved elsewhere to work as a yoga teacher.

John knew nothing of Sufism. He never came to the group meetings. But I wonder if his life would have undergone the same transformation if he had not been living next door to a group of love's drunkards?

The story of John is one example of the hidden influence of the hearts of His lovers. When a group meditates together the energy generated is more than the sum of its members. When ten people are sitting together the energy can be a hundred times as powerful as that of one person; and if their hearts are full of longing and cry for God it can be a thousand times as powerful.

Sufi groups have a particular potency because they are bonded together in love. Al-Hallâj says that "souls make cohorts; they form in groups according to their chosen affinities."[6] When the chosen affinity of souls is love's service they are a collective doorway for love to flow into the world. Their work is to keep aligned with the energy of the heart so that the doors of love can be kept open. The influence of such a group goes far beyond its immediate environment. They can have a direct influence upon the energy structure of the planet—help attune the world to love.[7]

SOLITUDE IN THE CROWD

His lovers learn to live in the two worlds, to be inwardly immersed in love and outwardly to work in the world. An important part of this process is the principle of "solitude in the crowd," which is one of the eight principles that form the basis of the Naqshbandi Path.[8] The essence of "solitude in the crowd" is: "In all your outward activity remain inwardly free. Learn not to identify yourself with anything whatsoever." There is a story about an early Sufi master, Khwâja 'Arîf Rîwgarî, that illustrates the degree of inner freedom that can result from such an attitude. Khwâja 'Arîf Rîwgarî was the fourth deputy of Khwâja 'Abd al-Khâliq Ghujduwânî, the twelfth-century master who set up the eight basic Naqshbandi principles and introduced the silent *dhikr*.[9] The chain of transmission from Bahâ' ad-dîn Naqshband goes back through 'Arîf Rîwgarî to 'Abd al-Khâliq Ghujduwânî.

When Chingis Khân invaded Turkestan his Mongol soldiers stopped at the village of Rîwgara, about twenty miles from Bukhârâ. Most of the villagers had fled in terror, but Khwâja 'Arîf was found working peacefully at his loom. An officer reported this unusual occurrence to Chingis Khân, who had the Khwâja brought to him. Chingis Khân asked him, through an interpreter, why he had not fled in terror like the other villagers. Khwâja 'Arîf simply replied, "My outer attention was on my work and my inner attention was on God; I have no time to notice what was happening in the world around me."

Chingis Khân was so impressed with this reply, and with the peace and tranquility of the Khwâja, that he ordered his soldiers to leave the village in peace, and he asked Khwâja 'Arîf to go with him to Bukhârâ and advise him whom he should trust. Unlike the people of the other cities which Chingis Khân captured, the inhabitants of Bukhârâ were not massacred.[10]

This story about Khwâja 'Arîf shows how an inner state of freedom allows a creative involvement in the outer world that is not determined by the patterns of the collective, by the desires, fears, and anxieties that so influence people's actions and way of life. Being unidentified with the outer world gives an individual the freedom to fully respond to the need of the moment, and, paradoxically, allows for a richer appreciation of life, as Irina Tweedie describes: "My life is at an end, but I tell you that flowers have never looked so red; nor has food tasted as good as it does now. And yet I am not chasing after these things, the things of the world. There is something else I cannot name which is lovelier still...."[11]

The practice of "solitude in the crowd" allows for an alignment with the essence rather than the form of life. Living in the world we do not identify with our actions but with the source from which they flow. The real work is to remain in tune with our inner nature, our natural way of being, whatever the pressures or attractions of the outer world. It is easy to be caught in a collective current of desire or anxiety, that, for example, may influence us to think that we may be happier with a new car or make us worry about the future. The more we identify with our inner essence the more we are able to appreciate how it is the source of real nourishment; the loaves and fishes with which Christ fed the five thousand symbolize the inner wisdom that comes from the unconscious, and there is always enough to go around.

Life becomes poverty-stricken when it is not lived from the source. When we are out of alignment with our inner self nothing that the world has to offer will satisfy our hunger. Yet we live in an age which tells us that fulfillment and happiness come from the external, material world. This is reflected in the amusing anecdote of a film star who had been brought up in poverty. A year or so after becoming famous and wealthy he said that he was surprised that he still had "down days." His innocent disconcertion points to the power of a collective conditioning which both imprisons and starves our culture.

The limitations of form and the danger of judging by outer circumstances are illustrated in a Taoist story about a farmer whose horse ran away:

> The farmer's neighbor, hearing about the runaway horse, came to commiserate, only to be told, "Who knows what's good or bad?" The next day the horse returned, bringing with it a herd of wild horses which it had befriended in its wanderings. The neighbor came over again, this time to congratulate the farmer on his windfall. He was met with the same observation: "Who knows what is good or bad?" True this time too; the next day the farmer's son tried to mount one of the wild horses and fell off, breaking his leg. Back came the neighbor, this time with more commiserations, only to encounter for the third time the same response, "Who knows what is good or bad?" And once

again the farmer's philosophical answer proved correct, for the next day soldiers came by commandeering for the army and because of his injury, the son was not drafted.[12]

The story continues, not only illustrating the relativity of good and bad, but also how things turn into their opposite.

MATRIARCHAL THINKING

Through the practice of "solitude in the crowd" the wayfarer learns not to be attached to any form. The state of inner freedom resulting from a lack of attachment to any outer situation enables the wayfarer to flow with the change, and thus to allow outer circumstances to reveal their inner potential. The soul has a very different set of criteria from the ego's, and what from an outer perspective can appear a disastrous situation may offer a tremendous potential for transformation. Recently a friend was confronted with the possibility of losing his house and his inheritance through a financial disaster outside of his control, a financial disaster that affected many people besides himself and his family. Just as this situation came to light he had a dream in which he was about to sell an empty house, but all that was left was a giant boa constrictor in the corner of a room. The boa was hungry and therefore dangerous. The dreamer thought of going to get the snake some food, but then felt just to watch and follow the snake. The dream ended with the snake transforming into a beautiful large eagle, which alighted on the dreamer's wrist like a falcon.

This dream tells the dreamer that if he just watches

the inner and outer dynamic evoked by this financial disaster, the unconscious feelings—the hungry snake—will not strangle and consume him, but rather be transformed into an eagle, which traditionally is the only bird that can look directly into the sun without blinking. The eagle symbolizes the spiritual energy of the Self, the philosophical gold, which is made from the undifferentiated energy of the unconscious. Jung writes that "in the alchemical process the *serpents mercurialis*, the dragon, is changed into the eagle..."[13]

The boa constrictor belongs to the jungle, to the instinctual depths within us. It is the primal energy of life, but being undifferentiated it knows neither good nor evil, and can only too easily overwhelm us, swallow us back into the darkness of the primordial night. But through the inner alchemical process, the inner work, this energy is transformed into consciousness, and the snake becomes an eagle which the dreamer will be able to master as a falconer masters a falcon. In Sufi symbolism the falcon is the bird of the soul "who is captured in the cold, dark, shadow world in the midst of ravens and crows, and is finally called back to God with the Qur'anic word *irji'î*, 'Come back, O soul at peace!'" (Sura 89:27).[14]

The dreamer's conditioning would make him try to alleviate the outer situation, to become involved in trying to save his inheritance, but the dream suggests that the best approach is not to find food to feed the hungry snake—all the fears, anxieties, and feelings evoked by the disaster—but just to watch these feelings. This is the ancient art of "work without doing," which Eric Neumann calls "matriarchal consciousness."[15] Matriarchal consciousness, which Neumann suggests is an older mode of thought than the rational, analytic mode, is an attitude of receptivity in which one

watches the processes of the unconscious, one's feelings and dream images. Matriarchal thinking belongs
to the right side of the brain and is holistic rather than
the left brain's analytic mode. Matriarchal thinking
does not attempt to dissect or rationalize. It is exhibited
by the Australian aborigines, who in their over three
hundred distinct languages have no word for time, and
who describe things analogically, according to their
similarities and correspondences rather than their
differences. Underlying and antecedent to the aborigines' outer reality is the "Dreaming," the all-pervading
consciousness that has a symbolic nature, and is similar
to our concept of the unconscious. Apparently their
figurative art, depicting animals, is a recent development. Their traditional art consisted of geometric
patterns, but because white man couldn't read this
symbolic language they developed a representational
iconography to communicate with the "civilized"
world.[16]

Matriarchal consciousness allows for the forma-
tion of symbols and, as such, a symbolic relationship
to life. An American Indian, Chief Luther Standing
Bear, describes how this ancient mode of thinking
connected man to the sacred rhythm of life:

> The man who sat on the ground in front of his
> tipi meditating on life and its meaning, accept-
> ing the kinship of all creatures and acknowledg-
> ing unity with the universe of things, was
> infusing into his being the true essence of
> civilization. And when native man left off this
> form of development, his humanization was
> retarded in growth.[17]

Matriarchal consciousness also allows for wholeness and harmony. In our Western world it has been repressed by the increasing dominance of analytical, directed thinking. Matriarchal thinking has been devalued, and for the majority it exists unrecognized in the unconscious, expressing itself only in dreams, fantasies, and vague feelings. That matriarchal thinking can be so suppressed has recently been corroborated by the neurological discovery that the left hemisphere can repress or inhibit the activities, and especially the emotionally-toned activities, of the right hemisphere. [18] If we are to live in harmony with our deepest nature, we must reclaim this holistic mode of thinking.

The attitude of receptivity, of "watching" or "witnessing," supports the work of inner transformation without interfering:

> Less and less is done until nothing is done
> When nothing is done, nothing is left undone. [19]

Through watching and accepting our feelings, dream images, and symbols, we add the important catalyst of consciousness to the process of transformation. This conscious participation in the process is an act of awareness, rather than action, that allows the seed of the Self to germinate into consciousness.

The work of the dreamer was just to watch and follow the snake and thus let the inner process take its course without his interfering. This necessitates a degree of trust and surrender that can be very threatening to ego-consciousness. But in learning to surrender to this process we not only create a space for our own numinous nature to manifest, we also gradually attune our consciousness to the inner world. Matriarchal consciousness allows for a symbolic relationship to life in which the meaning of one's outer life is not dependent on outer situations but on the inner whole-

ness of the Self. The Self has a wholeness and completeness that is beyond the comprehension of the ego,
and only by learning to live in harmony with its inner
rhythm can we allow this deeper unity to become a
part of our everyday life.

However, in order to allow the inner processes to
mature we need to be detached. The dreamer had to
be detached from any sense of security offered by his
prospective inheritance. Otherwise his attachment
would hold him in a desire to try to rectify the situation,
and he could easily then be crushed and swallowed by
the hungry boa constrictor. Rather than being able to
watch the inner dynamic he would be a victim of his
fears and desires.

Yet at the same time this does not mean that one
has to be entirely inactive; it means simply that one's
actions should not be driven by anxiety or fear. Khwâja
'Arif did not run away in fear of the Mongol horde, and
was thus able to creatively participate in a very
dangerous collective situation. A state of inner freedom enables us to flow with the changing situations of
life, rather than hanging on to old patterns which are
often destroyed by the new.

The more we focus on the inner rather than the
outer the less we are attached to form and the more our
attention is held by the real substance of life. Forms are
by their very nature containers of past situations. As we
inwardly grow and expand, past forms can become
limiting, as Christ expressed when he said that if you
put new wine into old bottles, "the bottles break, and
the wine runneth out."[20] But we do not need to look for
a new form, because as the energy of life manifests it
attracts the form it needs at that moment. This is a
dynamic and fluid process which runs counter to all
our patterns of conditioning that make us believe that

security is defined by the container, that the more established the container is the greater the security it offers.

We have our own personal forms, our patterns of behavior and value systems. But deeper and more ingrained are the collective patterns which appear to offer an even greater security. Nationalism is one example of a collective identity that seems to offer security; and yet at the same time the drive to protect this identity can result in tribe- or race-motivated aggression, and in the worst cases war. This type of security evokes fear and then too easily catches the individual in a collective shadow dynamic, which can have destructive results.

First the seeker must confront the personal shadow, what we repress into our unconscious. But the path of individuation then takes us deeper into the realms of the collective shadow. And just as our personal shadow is usually encountered through an outer situation that evokes unpleasant feelings like anger, jealousy, or greed, so too can the collective shadow be confronted through an outer situation. In the experience encountered by the dreamer a collective fear was actually aroused because not only he but also many other people involved in this financial disaster faced losing everything. The collective nature of this inner dynamic was suggested by the size of the boa constrictor. Such a giant snake belongs to the archetypal world, and can be evoked by a collective drama. The dreamer's "inheritance" would confront him with feelings, attachments, and fears belonging not only to his family but to his social class.

The friend who watched the boa constrictor had to confront not only his personal financial loss, but the deeper collective fear. If a culture stresses the security offered by money, then its shadow—the fear of losing money—is a powerful monster lurking in the depths.[21] However, the collective shadow cannot be confronted until much work has been done on the personal shadow. If the dreamer had still been caught in the shadowland of personal attachments he would have been swallowed by the collective fear. Our own personal shadow can easily pull us into the darker depths of the collective, as, for example, when the fear or experience of unemployment awakens the monster of racism and immigrants become blamed for both personal and national problems.

But this dream begins with a house which is empty of everything except the snake. To empty the house of one's psyche is a long and painstaking work, but only when it is empty can the deepest transformation take place. We work hard to empty ourself of ourself, because only then can the real mystery of a human being take place:

> Try and be a sheet of paper with nothing on it.
> Be a spot of ground where nothing is growing,
> where something might be planted,
> a seed, possibly, from the Absolute.[22]

WATCHERS OF THE CURRENT

We belong to the Beloved. Slowly we are made empty so that we can be attentive to His needs. Inwardly we learn to be receptive and wait, like a cat at a mouse hole, infinitely relaxed and infinitely alert. We watch our inner self, our dreams and intuitions. Both detached and observant we watch the outer world. In this way we learn to watch the flow of life as it comes into the world. We move with the flow; unattached to forms we respond to the moment. We are attuned with life before it manifests because we are attuned to the source of life and our hearts are open to the current of love that is life's essence.

Watching our dreams we learn to move with this current. Dreams so often describe an inner dynamic that underlies what is manifest. If we are in harmony with this inner dynamic we become in harmony with life and the hidden meaning of life. The friend who dreamt of the snake transforming into an eagle was able to consciously orient himself so that he could grasp the inner potential of the outer situation.

Usually events constellate on the inner planes before they manifest in the outer world. If we are in harmony with our inner self, if we are inwardly attentive, then we come into harmony with events before they manifest. Dreams often inwardly align us and when we share dreams within a group we share this inner alignment and have it reinforced by others. In this way we work together, helping each other and creating a group space where the outer and inner are aligned. A protected space develops within the group consciousness where the inner and outer worlds meet and are in harmony. The inner is allowed to manifest without the resistance it often encounters, without the crystallized patterns of thought and behavior that can so easily pollute the pure flow of the waters of life.

Standing on the edge of the beyond we welcome the beyond. We embrace the unexpected and merge into life's essence. This creates a dynamic center in which the energy of life can come freely into the world and bring its potential wholeness. Life in its essence is always whole. It is only ego-consciousness that contaminates this wholeness, accepting what fits into its prescribed patterns and rejecting what it considers unacceptable. But if we are focused on the Self rather than the ego, if we are attentive in our inner attitude to life's flow rather than to our desires, then we create a space where life's potency and primal wholeness can flow freely.

Our dreams are born from our own wholeness. So often they include what we reject, and point us back to the Self. Listening to our dreams we listen to the song of the deeper self, and allow the deeper self to be heard. We create a bridge that links the inner world of the psyche with an outer world that has been cut off from the natural rhythms of life and as a result has become dangerously fragmented. Dreams are not just images or pictures. They carry an energy that comes from the inner world, and through listening to them, through being attentive to their implications and the feelings they evoke, we allow this energy into consciousness. Working with our own dreams we open ourself to the transformative potential of our own inner being. Working with dreams as a group we allow the inner world to be impressed upon the group consciousness, subtly affecting the collective consciousness.

Listening to our dreams, discussing and trying to understand what they have to tell us, we engage our whole self in this mysterious process. Not only the mind, but the emotions, the feelings, and the depths of the heart are involved in dreamwork. The mystery of the inner world—of the shadow, the archetypes, and the golden child of the Self—becomes woven into the patterns of consciousness. The wonder of the transformation of a human being, the inner unfolding of the light hidden in darkness, gradually permeates the consciousness of the group. Each in our own way, according to our own receptivity, we absorb the miracle of opening, we sense the presence of the beyond.

Working with dreams we learn to work with the symbolic substance of life that underlies our own consciousness and also the collective consciousness of our culture. Individually and as a group we become watchers of the currents of the inner world. We learn to listen to and trust in these inner patterns of unfolding, so that we cooperate with our own process of transformation, and also with the deeper, collective processes that are shaping the destiny of the planet. Jung stresses that it is the collective archetypal energies that are the real determining factors:

> Our personal psychology is just a thin skin, a ripple on the ocean of collective psychology. The powerful factor, the factor which changes our whole life, which changes the surface of our known world, which makes history, is collective psychology, and collective psychology moves according to laws entirely different to those of our consciousness. The archetypes are the great decisive factors, they bring about real changes, and not our personal reasoning and practical intellect. The archetypal images decide the fate of man.[23]

As the Piscean era comes to an end and the age of Aquarius begins, a new archetype is constellating in the collective unconscious; a new way of relating to and experiencing our intrinsic wholeness is being born. This archetype is not a cross nor a circle, as in previous ages; it is not a form at all but a sacred space within which we are able to reconnect with our essence, a space which holds the connection between the Creator and His creation. In space everything merges and is united—we are a part of the one great whole; we can listen to the song of the whole of creation as His love is made manifest. The nature of this sacred space is that it is not defined by boundaries but rather by its quality of connection that allows us to feel and experience the unity of life. It is a space which allows us to be our own true self and to recognize the individuality of others. Within this space we feel the sacred wholeness of all life and at the same time the profound uniqueness of each particle of creation.

However, this newly emerging archetype is not yet fully present within our collective consciousness. Instead we seem to be confronted by the forms of a decaying culture and images empty of meaning:

A heap of broken images, where the sun beats,
And the dead tree gives no shelter, the cricket
    no relief,
And the dry stone no sound of water.[24]

Today's "dead trees" have no real fruit, offer no nourishment, but only consume our attention with their interminable problems. Old patterns must die for the new to be born, but it is these decaying patterns that are most visible. They are still in the forefront of consciousness because they are what we have been conditioned to notice and value. The new is often invisible because our mind only registers what it is programmed to record.

As a culture we are so conditioned by old patterns that we expect the future to be an elaboration of the past. We look for more technology and greater productivity. Even the "new age" culture often emphasizes the technology of self-transformation, the techniques of re-birthing or visualization. We expect spiritual change to follow similar patterns to those of our "scientific revolution," producing tangible results and verifiable improvements. Yet what is being born is something so new that it does not belong to the patterns of the past. It is born from the eternal present, from the moment outside of time, and is not a product of history. It is invisible because it does not have a definable form.

We are conditioned to value cultures by the monuments they leave behind, and thus judge the Greeks and the Romans by their temples and aqueducts. The limitation of this approach was tragically evident when the white people judged the Native American Indians to be ignorant savages because they lived "without leaving traces," in harmony with nature rather than trying to dominate their environment. It has taken a century or more to realize that the richness of the Indian culture can be found in their religious ceremonies and in their sacred relationship to the land. What if we are now being awakened into an age in which essence rather than form carries the value and potency? How will we notice what is happening and give ourself to this new unfolding? How can consciousness be prepared to witness this awakening?

As wayfarers on the mystical path we learn to welcome what we do not yet know—that which is coming from the beyond into consciousness. The new will always be threatening to those attached to the old ways, to the forms created in the past. Yet amidst the structures which have evolved from the past the present is dynamically alive as something new, not as a problem to be solved but as life giving of itself. This present is not delineated by forms but is found in the space that is permeated with life's essence. Space is the mystery of the feminine from which life is born and reborn. Space does not define and imprison, but allows. Space is permeated with meaning and real purpose:

> Thirty spokes share the wheel's hub;
> It is the center hole that makes it useful.
> Shape clay into a vessel;
> It is the space that makes it useful.
> Cut doors and windows for a room;
> It is the holes which make it useful.
> Therefore profit comes from what is there;
> Usefulness from what is not there.[25]

Identifying with form we have become isolated because forms are defined by their separateness. In space there is connection and movement. In space there is flow; and in its movement the magic of life is hidden. Feeling life's movement we sense the mystery of being and its continuous unfolding. Identifying with form, each time we arrive at a place we seek to define it, to pin it down. But the more we try to define life the more we lose its flow. Then instead of experiencing its energy and vitality, we become lost in a backwater that only gathers pollution.

Imprisoned in the forms we have created, in our technological towers and problem-solving mind-sets, we have already polluted the outer world. When life ceases to flow from the source, pollution results and problems abound. Rather than seeking a solution we need to open ourself so that life can flow freely. It is life flowing again from the source that will heal the earth, just as a human's life force is the prime agent in any healing. The new age which is unfolding is not a solution because it does not belong to any problem. It is rather an opening to the beyond, a doorway in time and space that connects us to the source from which all life comes.

THE THREAD OF UNION

His lovers are free of forms because they have merged with what is formless. Giving themselves in silence they have entered the arena of not being. In meditation the mind dissolves in the heart; the drop disappears in the ocean of love, and instead of form there is essence. It is essence that speaks to His lovers. It is for this they have abandoned the world. Walking the path of love His servants have become familiar with the inward, with the substance that underlies creation. They have glimpsed behind the veils of the world, seeing that "God does not look at outward forms, but at the love within your love."[26] It is this song of what is formless that His lovers sing in their everyday life. This is the gift they bring. This is the burden they bear.

Walking the loneliest of paths His wayfarers are familiar with the unknown and with unknowing. They are open to the unexpected because the ways of love are always unexpected. They can welcome the dawn because they are friends with the darkness of God. They have learned to wait for their Beloved, and in their waiting have become accustomed to silence, and in that silence have found the seeds of the future.

Lovers do not belong to time but to the tremendous presence of eternity. It is in remembrance of this timeless moment that they live their everyday life, with each breath repeating the *dhikr* that connects them with the time before time. Inwardly they hold together the threads of love that link the creation to the Creator, for they know in their hearts and their minds that in the whole universe all that exists is the lover and the Beloved. Even the cells of the body remember this secret from moments of intoxication and bliss. This secret His lovers hold in trust for the world, and standing on the edge of the beyond they witness His presence in both the silent emptiness of the inward and the kaleidoscopic tumult of the outward. They know that "everything is He."

Within a group of lovers this knowledge is the bond of the heart that underlies the purpose of being together. They meet to share this knowledge, to weave it into consciousness, for it is a hidden secret that desires to be known. This is the work they do for the world. It is the golden thread that runs through their dreams. It is the thread of their own deepest destiny.

Watching our dreams we learn to see how this thread is woven in both our inner and outer life. We become familiar with its texture and how it holds the tension of the two worlds. It is the path "as narrow as the edge of a razor" along which we must walk. It is the thread of union woven into the experience of separation.

Meeting together, sharing silence and the longing for truth, seekers create a space where the beyond is present and the unity of being permeates consciousness. Here the archetype of a sacred space is a lived reality, experienced by those who make their own inner journey in the company of friends. The inner journey takes us from separation to wholeness, from the ego to the Self. This journey is the unique expression of a human being because it is the inner essence being made conscious. The Sufi says that "There are as many ways to God as there are human beings, as many as the breaths of the children of men." Our own path is an offering of our own uniqueness back to the Great Artist in whose image we are made. For each of us the path will be different. It will carry the stamp of our individual relationship with the Beloved. And yet at the same time within a spiritual group this is a shared journey. Together we form a caravan of souls going home.

A spiritual group offers both intimacy and aloneness. It is a space within which we can work towards uncovering our own essential nature, "the face we had before we were born." The group is a container for this work. It provides a secure space in the world which values the individual relationship of the soul to God, and the ways in which the outer world and everyday life can help us to uncover this innermost secret of the heart:

> You may be happy enough going along,
> but with others you'll get farther and faster.
>
> Someone who goes cheerfully by himself
> to the customs house to pay his traveller's tax
> will go even more lightheartedly
> when friends are with him.
>
> Every prophet sought out companions.
> A wall standing alone is useless,
> but put three or four walls together,
> and they'll support a roof and keep
> the grain dry and safe.[27]

In the sacred space of the group our own sacred nature is held safe. This is not the safety of outer security which so easily constellates into its opposite, fear. This is the safety of the Self and love's intimacy. It is the safety of those who give themselves to God and allow Him into their lives, a safety born of abandonment and matured in detachment. Only in the emptiness of God is there real security, and the sign of this security is spiritual poverty: "The reality of poverty is that one becomes rich through God alone; its outer guise is non-attention to ways and means."[28]

When a spiritual group lives this sacred space and experiences its potency and potential for growth, this new archetype is gradually integrated into the collective consciousness. Spiritual seekers have always stood at the forefront of emerging patterns of consciousness, because they are friends with the unknown from which the new emerges into consciousness. Free from the attachments of the old, seekers are used to welcoming the new, just as the wise men of the East welcomed the newborn Christ.

A spiritual group is in itself a doorway to the beyond, a space in which grace flows into the world. When seekers come together for the sole purpose of going Home, this grace is channeled. It is present in the meditation and the sharing of hearts. It gives us the energy and help we need to complete the impossible task. Through it what is new and hidden is able to become manifest, within the individual, within the group, and within the collective consciousness. In previous ages stone circles, temples, and churches provided the sacred spaces for the inner essence, the energy of the beyond, to flow into the world. Groups are the archetypal containers for the work of the future. It is here that the secrets of the coming age will be shared.

THE PEOPLE OF THE SECRET

I saw my Lord with the eye of the heart
And said: "Who are you?" He answered: "You!"
Al-Hallâj[1]

LOVE'S MARTYR

In 922 A.D., Husain ibn Mansûr al-Hallâj was executed in Baghdad, and became love's martyr. Like the ninth-century ecstatic Bâyezîd Bistâmî, who exclaimed, "Glory be to Me! How great is my glory!" al-Hallâj not only inwardly experienced but outwardly spoke the tremendous mystical truth of the lover's annihilation in the Beloved. Louis Massignon, who devoted his whole life to the study of al-Hallâj, has shown that it was not so much his famous statement, *anâ'l-haqq,* "I am the Absolute Truth," that condemned him, as some of his religious theories. However, through his death al-Hallâj became celebrated throughout the Islamic world as a great lover, as the one who "without fear divulged the secret of the unity of man and God."[2]

Al-Hallâj welcomed his execution because he knew that death leads to the final union of the lover and the Beloved. Before the flagellation that preceded his execution he said:

> Kill me, O my faithful friends
> for to kill me is to make me live;
> My life is my death, and my death is my life.[3]

Then just before he died he exclaimed, "My God, here I am now in the dwelling place of my desires."[4] Al-Hallâj knew love's truth and witnessed it before the vast crowd that had gathered to see his execution. He physically enacted the reality of the heart in which the lover ceases to exist in the state of union with God. He was prepared to pay the price of his own life to make public this innermost mystery.

Al-Hallâj's death was the final statement of what he had publicly preached in Baghdad. Speaking to ordinary people at the entrance to a mosque, he said:

> O people! When Truth has taken hold of a heart, She empties it of all but Herself! When God attaches Himself to a man, He kills in him all else but Himself![5]

and on another occasion in the marketplace, he was heard saying:

> I have embraced, with my whole being, all Your love, O my Holiness! You have manifested Yourself so much that it seems to me that there is only You in me!
>
> I examine my heart amidst all that is not You.
>
> I do not see any estrangement between them and me, and only familiarity between You and me![6]

Al-Hallâj, immersed in the states of nearness, only asked that, "You do not return me to myself, after having robbed me of myself."[7] And years before his execution he entered a mosque and told a crowd that the spilling of his blood was lawful, for then he would have gained peace and died a martyr.[8]

Many of the Sufis of the time disagreed with al-Hallâj's ecstatic utterances. Al-Junayd, one of the foremost Sufis who taught in Baghdad and advocated a path of sobriety, supposedly rejected al-Hallâj from his circle, saying "I do not accept madmen." Yet the truth of the union with the Beloved is known to all mystics. Al Junayd depicts the same death that al-Hallâj enacted when he describes the state of *fanâ*: "God possesses him [the saint] with a supreme violence; He reduces him to dust before he dies; He kills him, buries him; then, if it pleases Him, He resuscitates him.... this death is his access to the arena of primordial Life."[9] But al-Junayd and other Sufis felt that this process of transformation and the mystery of Oneness should be kept a secret. What was known in the heart and shared in the circle of friends was not to be told in the marketplace.

Because al-Hallâj told what should be kept secret he was put to death. Even al-Hallâj's friend al-Shiblî said this at the time of the execution: "God gave you access to one of His secrets, but because you made it public, He has made you taste the blade."[10] Later al-Shiblî is supposed to have said that "this man has shown what had remained concealed from creatures; and had he not been in a hurry he would have had a happy life."[11]

But it is also told that on the day "when that prince of lovers, Mansûr [al-Hallâj], was crucified," al-Shiblî said in a dream to God:

"Why do you put your lovers to death?"
"So that they may receive blood-money from Me."
"Lord, what is your blood-money?"
"To find me and see My beauty—that is the blood-money of My lovers."[12]

To dare to die for love is to be embraced by the Beloved, and God's promise to be the blood-money for those who have been slain by love for Him became a *hadîth qudsî* (extra-Qur'anic revelation) celebrating the mystic's death in love. Al-Hallâj became the hero of lovers who long for their Beloved more than reason, and wish only to offer themselves on the sacrificial altar of their hearts, as Rûmî exclaims: "The lovers walk gladly to the gallows like Mansûr!"[13]

THE NATURE OF LONGING

Through the actions of al-Hallâj the mysteries of love became known in the market and the mosque. He honored the suffering known to those who seek what cannot be found and are burnt by the invisible fire of longing. He knew the depths of the suffering of love, "which exceeds the forces of created nature," and knew this suffering as a sign of His closeness, for "Suffering is Himself, while good fortune comes from Him."[14]

This intense inner longing is the central core of every mystical path, as the anonymous author of the fourteenth-century mystical classic, *The Cloud of Unknowing,* simply states: "Your whole life must be one of longing." Yet our present Western society is so divorced from this mystical thread that underlies every spiritual path that we have no context within which to appreciate the nature of the heart's desire for Truth. There are many people who feel the unhappiness of a homesick soul, and yet do not know its cause. They do not realize the wonder of their pain, or that it is this, their heart's longing, that will take them Home.

A friend had a simple and powerful dream in which she was alone in a landscape, howling at the moon. There was no reply, no answer to the anguish of her calling, and when she awoke she felt a failure. She had called out and there had been no answer. But the tradition of lovers has long known that our calling is the answer, our longing for Him is His longing for us—"it is You who calls me to Yourself." The longing of the heart is the memory of when we were together with Him. In this memory there is no duality, only union. The lover and the Beloved are one, and so when we feel the pain of separation it is His pain we honor in our hearts.

The longing of the heart is the sign of the deepest fulfillment, and yet it terrifies the mind because it does not belong to this world. There is no visible lover, no one to touch or to control. It is a love affair of essence to essence that was born before the beginning of time. Sadly, we have forgotten its potency; our culture has no place for this desire for what is intangible. In the Christian tradition this relationship is embodied in Mary Magdalene's devotion for Christ. After the crucifixion she stood at the empty sepulchre, where he had been buried, weeping. And when Jesus, risen from the dead, came and spoke to her, saying, "Woman, why weepest thou? Whom seekest thou?" She first mistook him for a gardener until he called her by name, "Mary," and then she "turned herself and said 'Rabboni, which is to say, Master.'"[15]

In this meeting there are longing and devotion and the ancient mystery of the relationship of teacher and disciple. It has been often overlooked that Mary Magdalene was the first to see the risen Christ, but it is deeply significant; for it is this inner attitude of the heart, of longing and devotion, that she embodies, that opens the lover to the transcendent mystery of love in which suffering and death are the doorway to a higher state of consciousness. The lover waits weeping for the Beloved to reveal His true nature.

Our culture has forgotten and buried the doorway of devotion, and the lover is often left stranded, not even knowing the real nature and purpose of the longing that tugs at the heart. It is easy to think that this discontent of the soul is a psychological problem and identify it as a mother complex or the result of an unhappy marriage. We need to reclaim the sanctity of sadness and the meaning of the heart's tears. For the longing of the lover is a longing to return to the source in which everything is embraced in its wholeness. The suffering of His lovers is the labor pain that awakens us to this higher consciousness, in which love joins this world with the infinite, and the heart embraces life not from the divisive perspective of the ego but from the eternal dimension of the Self. From within the heart the oneness of love becomes life's deepest wonder, for "It is the heart that sees the primordial eternity of every creature."[16]

If we can create a context of longing then those whose hearts are burdened with this quest will come to know the true nature of their pain. They will no longer need to repress it, fearing it as an abnormality or a psychological problem. We need to be able to collectively affirm this inner secret: that the heart suffers because it has not forgotten its true love.

Longing is the pain of separation and at the same time the affirmation of union. It is the dynamic imprint upon consciousness of the soul's memory of the eternal moment when we are together with God. Each moment of longing reminds us of our real nature, and the more potent this pain is the more this memory is alive within the heart. Thus the work of a mystic is to keep this fire burning within the heart, and through devotion and aspiration to let it burn so strongly that it burns away the veils of separation. Then the memory of union becomes a living reality within the heart of the lover. In the fire and pain of this longing the imprisoning walls of the ego gradually dissolve until the eternal moment of the Self can be lived in full consciousness. The Beloved becomes no longer just a hint hidden within the heart, but a constant Companion and Friend.

ROMANCE AND MYSTICAL LOVE

We live in an age and society which celebrate romantic love but have buried and forgotten the deeper mystical love that underlies every love affair. The ideal of romance burst into our Western culture in the Middle Ages with the love songs of the troubadours and then became formulated in the medieval code of courtly love in which the lover is always obedient to his beloved. The troubadour love songs were born from the meeting of East and West at the time of the crusades. Their origin can be traced to the Middle East, and to the symbolic, mystical poetry of the Sufis. Love's sorrow as sung by the Sufis belongs to the beyond:

> Inspired by love's sorrow, the minstrel sang out
> Such an ode that the eyelashes of the world's
> Philosophers streamed tears of blood.[17]

These Sufi poets wrote of the beauty of their beloved, of how they were made drunk by the ringlets of her hair and devastated by her bewitching eye, of how her eyelashes left the poet's heart bathed in blood while her chin enravished the world's heart. But the beloved that these poets adored was not to be found in the outer world. She who is eternally present is hidden and invisible, as Hâfez describes:

> O lord of love, to whom can I tell
> Such subtle love-lore, who cares to listen?
> That everywhere-wandering mistress,
> That divine witness of the heart,
> Never once showed her features to anyone![18]

Our Western culture is saturated with the images of romantic love in films and songs, and yet we have lost contact with the mystical roots of the heart's longing for another. We project all our desires for fulfillment on the outer world, not realizing that the bliss we desire belongs to the soul. Romantic love captivates us because it is a thread that comes from the beyond. But because our society has dismissed the inner world, we are left with the echo of love's promise, and only too easily is romance debased into emotion or physical passion.

We need to reclaim longing and own its potency and purpose. We need to affirm the spiritual roots of love so that those who desire something more than the outer world know the substance of their discontent and do not confuse it with depression. The same secret that al-Hallâj told in the markets and mosques of Baghdad needs to be shared today, so that the thread of love can be rewoven into the collective consciousness.

SHARING THE SECRETS OF LOVE

At times the ways of the heart need to be kept hidden so that His lovers will not be persecuted. This was possibly one of the reasons that al-Junayd rejected the "madman" al-Hallâj. For centuries Sufis have been the people of the secret, using cryptic language to describe the nature of mystical love. They describe the journey to the invisible Beloved in terms of the attractions and attributes of a physical beloved, whose tresses become "a place of profoundest mysteries,"[19] whose cheek "represents the beauty of *Lâ ilâha illâ llâh* (There is no God but God)"[20], and whose beauty spot symbolizes the Divine Essence itself which cannot be fathomed:

> From her beauty spot stems
> All the grief and blood that brims
> within our hearts;
> No way out, no exit
> From this degree exists.[21]

Mysticism is paradoxical by nature and easily misunderstood. Even when there is no fear of persecution mystics often prefer to be silent rather than to confuse others or evoke unnecessary arguments or confrontations. Instead they say "those who know, know and those who understand, understand." Aware that His mystery can never be described with words, they remain silent and perform their work of loving without the interference of others. This is the advice of the eleventh-century Sufi, Ansârî, in his devotional work *Munâjât,* "Intimate Conversations:"

> Strive to become the true human being:
> one who knows love, one who knows pain.

Be full, be humble, be utterly silent,
be the bowl of wine passed from hand to hand.[22]

But as the keepers of the secrets of love His lovers
need to keep open the gates of the heart and at times
remind the world that the mystery of creation is love,
"the essence of the divine essence."[23] These secrets of
the heart are like seeds that germinate in the darkness,
but there comes the time for opening, for the world to
see and recognize the beauty of its own flowering.

We live in an age when the spiritual nature of love
has been so forgotten that seekers are often left
stranded on the shores of this world, not even knowing
that within their hearts is the thread that will guide
them from separation to unity. Just as the inner world
needs to become part of our collective consciousness,
so too do the ways of love need to be brought into the
open.

Yet at the same time if we share these secrets in an
unwelcoming place, their subtleties can be lost and
their purpose easily polluted. Worse still the negativity
of the reception can attack the one who shares these
secrets, creating doubt and disbelief in place of wonder. Christ expressed these dangers when he said:

> Give not that which is holy unto the dogs,
> neither cast ye your pearls before swine, lest
> they trample them under their feet, and turn
> again and rend you.[24]

Our present social environment is so conditioned to
value only the ego and the outer world of sensations
that it can be an aggressively unsympathetic arena for
any perspective that goes beyond this pre-defined
horizon. I once experienced the way that the collective

can react when I spoke at a seminar about the transformative nature of suffering, which I found evoked an anger and hostility from the audience. Only later did I discover that in the audience was a large group of women who had joined together in a shared sense that they had been abused by men. They had become identified with their suffering and were not open to the idea that their suffering could have a transformative quality, and that they could move beyond it. The fact that I was a man only increased the level of angry rejection.

This experience illustrates the way the collective can react, and because this reaction is often unconscious it can have a direct effect upon the inner world. If we encounter a conscious reaction, a direct criticism, a verbal rejection or even attack, we are able to consciously distance ourself from another's negativity. But when we evoke an unconscious hostility we often lack the conscious awareness of what is happening and so absorb the negativity. If we are encountering a collective shadow-dynamic this negativity can be particularly damaging to a newly awakened inner awareness, which is often accompanied by vulnerability and insecurity. The rational disbelief of others is like a cold sword that cuts through the tender connection with the reality of the heart.

Discrimination is one of the most important spiritual qualities, and it is usually learned through painful mistakes. But if we are able to listen with the heart, with our feelings, then we come to know when an environment is sympathetic and open. If we listen to our own inner secret then it will tell us when it needs to be shared. So often a dream will wait for a particular moment to be told, and even the dreamer can be surprised to find himself telling it. The same is true of the secrets of the heart. They know when they are needed, and as much as we have to learn when to be silent so too do we have to be free of any imposed restraint. Once a friend was going to pick up her children from school and she started a brief conversation with another mother in the school parking lot. The mother was telling her that she was suffering from a painful physical and psychological condition and didn't know what to do. To her own surprise my friend began to tell about the meditation of the heart that we practice. In the middle of the school parking lot she outlined the meditation, and at the same time was thinking that this was hardly the place to share something so sacred. But then the children came out of school and the conversation was over. That evening the mother rang her in deep gratitude saying that after she had gotten home and her children were busy she had gone to her room and tried the meditation. She immediately went off in meditation and the pain left her!

The ways of the heart are not the ways of the mind and cannot be bound by any conditioning, because the nature of the heart is free. The heart is not limited by time, space, or any form. Sometimes, seekers carry a spiritual conditioning that is also a constriction, telling them what is and what is not spiritually appropriate. But as I was once told in a dream, "You cannot walk the path of straight with rules." Like the sunshine, the secrets of the heart are free and are to be shared freely when the need arises. The moment you apply rules you limit, and the heart belongs to the limitless ocean of love. Learning to share the secrets of love is to give yourself into the arms of the Self. In the words of Abû Sa'îd ibn Abî-l Khayr:

What you have in your head, forget it.
What you have in your hand, give it.
That which is to be your fate, face it!"

THE FEMININE MYSTERIES OF LOVE

Longing is the feminine side of love, the cup waiting to be filled. Longing is a highly dynamic state and yet at the same time it is a state of receptivity. Because our culture has for so long rejected the feminine we have lost touch with many of the subtleties of the feminine qualities of love. While we understand the instinctual nurturing of the mother, we have dismissed the attitude of receptivity which is needed in order to be responsive to another's needs. Just as this aspect of love is needed to nurture an outer child, it is also necessary for nurturing the child of the Self. We wait for the Beloved and in waiting we attune ourself to love's needs.

Love needs to be listened to with an attentive inner ear. This is not a state of passivity but of giving oneself to the needs of another. If we listen with our whole self we give ourself. We surrender to the mystery of our own heart and allow something greater than the ego to be born into consciousness. It is through this state of surrender that we are taken into the inner arena of love where we are transformed, where we are opened to the beyond.

A human relationship is often a wonderful opportunity to begin to learn to listen to love. If two people love each other there is a connection from heart to heart, from soul to soul. This is not to be confused with attachment or co-dependency. The difference is that in love there is space. When there is love between two people there is space and it is in that space that one can become familiar with the ways of love. In *The Prophet,* Kahlil Gibran writes:

> Love one another, but make not a bond of love:
> Let it be rather a moving sea between the shores
> of your soul.

In the space between two souls love flows; there is out-breathing and in-breathing, time to be together and time to be alone. It is in the space between two people that the real magic of a relationship takes place, because it is in space that the eternal unfolds into time. This vital space where hearts meet is the sacred space of any relationship; without it there are only the dynamics of projection and desire. Sadly, this sacred space is often unrecognized and overshadowed by the more visible demands of the ego, the fear of aloneness, and the complex patterns of our conditioning. Yet if we give ourself to the love dynamic of a relationship rather than just to our own needs and desires we can discover this place of real meeting.

Sufis say that just as playing with dolls prepares young girls to become mothers one day, so do human relationships prepare us for the real love affair with the Beloved. In the meeting place of human lovers the thread of a deeper love affair is hidden, and through listening and being receptive to another's heart, we become familiar with the "moving sea" of love. We come to the door of the heart of hearts where He is waiting.

Yet in this ultimate relationship there is not a meeting of two souls, but a merging into oneness. The Greatest Lover is the innermost part of our own being, "closer to you than yourself to yourself." While in any human love affair there is always the separateness of individuals—however close we are to another we are always two—with the Beloved there is the indescribable intimacy of oneness:

> You run between the heart and its sheath
> As tears run from the eyelids.[25]

The kiss this Lover brings to us is not on the lips, but on the *inside of the heart*. There is no meeting of bodies or separation of personalities. The whole relationship takes place in the hidden recesses of the heart, in that infinite inner space from which love unfolds into the world.

Spiritual life is a gift. We are taken to God because He wants to give Himself to us. Our work is to be open to this gift, to be waiting for the Beloved when He knocks on the door of our heart and comes to take us Home. Our masculine culture has been so identified with effort and will that we easily think that spiritual life is wholly dependent upon our own efforts. Spiritual life does require the most intense effort, but as Bâyezîd Bistâmî discovered, His love for us underlies all our searching:

> At the beginning I was mistaken in four respects. I concerned myself to remember God, to know Him, to love Him and to seek Him. When I had come to the end I saw that He had remembered me before I remembered Him, that His knowledge of me had preceded my knowledge of Him, that His love towards me had existed before my love to Him and He had sought me before I sought Him.[26]

We need to know that His love is the root of our longing, of our desire to return Home. If we give ourself to His love for His servant, then the inner chamber of the heart opens and He infuses us with the colorless fragrance of union. Inwardly it is a process of seduction. He, the great Beloved, the Master of the ways of love, seduces us with the scent of oneness. He calls us to Him, mysteriously turning our attention away from the outer world to the secrets of the soul, enticing us to the annihilation that every lover experiences in the moment of bliss.

THE SECRET OF SEDUCTION

In the following dream the dreamer is so conditioned to the thorny path of effort that she misses the moment of seduction and loses her way:

> Maggie, a serious young girl with flaming red hair, has a dream about me which is too passionate for her to tell me. Her mother, Grace, tells me that it is a dream about me and a man whom I love very much, Naqshbandi.
>
> I go to the house of a male friend who will take me to someone who can explain the dream to me, or even to Naqshbandi himself. I am so happy, flushed with anticipation and eager to be with him. Then I am with two male friends walking up a street in medieval England. The street is narrow, made of cobblestones, and lathe-and-plaster buildings are on either side. I hear our footsteps on the stones, I see the boards covering sewerage on the side of the road, and smell it and feel the cool dark street.

There is laundry hanging above us. I am walking ahead of them, I am so eager.

Then in one building I see that a second story is being added, and the framing is up, the framing of a window which will look out and down to the street. There are two young women up there on a bed, calling down to the people on the street. They are dressed in white skirts and tight bodices, lifting their round breasts. They are plump, round, and fun-looking. They are calling down to my two male companions things like, "Ooo, aren't you a cute one," and commenting to each other good-naturedly about them.

I look up and notice them and think that they are having fun. But I am focused on going to find Naqshbandi and keep going awhile before I realize that my two male friends are no longer with me, and I know that they have gone up to those two young women.

I am not surprised, and I think to myself that I'll just go back to my friend's house and wait for them so that I can be shown the way to Naqsh-bandi. I turn left into a very narrow, dim alley, and realize that I am now barefoot. I step into the alley and see that it is completely covered with thistles that are beautiful but spiny. I begin to walk down the alley, and with each step the thistles get caught in my feet. They do not cause me any pain and I just take them out after each step, looking at them before the next step.

This dream begins with a young girl, Maggie, whose flaming red hair suggests a fiery nature that is hidden beneath her "serious" demeanor. She has a dream that is too passionate to share and can only tell it to her mother Grace. This is a dream about a love affair with a man called Naqshbandi, which is the name of the Naqshbandi Sufi Path. Because our culture is so divorced from the ways of the soul, we have identified passion with sensuality, or even lust, and lost its deeper dimension. We speak of Christ's "passion" but reject the passionate nature of the soul's hunger for God. We are often embarrassed, ashamed, or even afraid of our own passion, particularly where there is a puritanical collective conditioning, as in North America.

To associate spirituality and passion is an inherited taboo. Yet the mystical relationship with God is an all-embracing ecstasy, a love affair of the soul. We long for Him with more tears and burning than any human lover can evoke, and the union He offers can have the intensity of every cell in orgasm and the soul screaming with a bliss that seems too much to bear. Everything dissolves in this meeting, the lover is so lost in love that hardly a trace remains. For a moment of such intensity one would gamble away the whole world and only know the wonder of losing everything, even oneself.

The attraction of the mystical path is its intensity. It needs to be lived each moment, getting deeper and deeper, until, as Bhai Sahib told Irina Tweedie, "The time will come when one wishes that twenty-four hours should be twenty-five in order to love someone one hour more." This is the nature of the passionate dream dreamt by the girl with flaming red hair. It is a dream of opening to the mysteries of love's oneness, a dream that begins when an invisible, untouchable lover lures us into the deadly arena of our own heart.

For the wayfarer the path takes us to love, and the dreamer's love affair with Naqshbandi is this path unfolding within her heart. The path is a love affair. The Sufi tradition describes two aspects of the path, *sulûk* and *jadhba*. *Sulûk* is the process of actively setting out towards God—repentance, the work on the shadow, the focus on the *dhikr* and other elements that demand the utmost effort on the part of the wayfarer. But *jadhba* is the more passive, feminine way in which the wayfarer is attracted by God towards Him. The Sufi is chosen by God since he is loved by Him, and through His love the wayfarer's heart is freed from attachment to anything except God. On most Sufi paths the wayfarer begins with the work of *sulûk,* and only in the later stages does he arrive at *jadhba*. However, the Naqshbandi path begins with *jadhba,* which is reflected in the saying about the Naqshbandi path that "the end is present in the beginning."[27] Although *jadhba* is a priority on this path, it does not mean that the Sufi can do without *sulûk,* but that these two aspects of grace and effort are integrated from the very beginning.

The priority given to *jadhba* reflects the fact that it is His love that turns the heart of the wayfarer back to Him. The path begins with His love for His servant, and our recognition of this allows us to give ourself willingly into the arms of love. Because our culture has forgotten the mystical dimension of love it is necessary to consciously acknowledge His desire for us, and thus reclaim the grace that flows from this love affair.

In this dream about Naqshbandi, the dreamer finds herself walking up a street in medieval England, with sewerage running through the open drains and laundry hanging above. The dreamer is happy, eager about the possibility of being with the man Naqshbandi whom she loves so much. She is being led by two male friends and they come to a building on which a second story is being added. In the window of the second story two sensual women are lying on a bed and call enticingly down. The dreamer notices that they are having fun but is too focused on her quest for Naqshbandi to be diverted and keeps on down the street, only to realize after a while that her two male guides are no longer with her. Then she turns left and finds herself in a street full of thorns.

Al-Hallâj says that God takes us to Him "either by a lure that seduces or by the violence that forces ... and God shows better through that which seduces, for a lure is superior to violence."[28] The scene enacted in the dream with the buxom women calling down to the men is an archetypal picture of seduction. The Beloved calls us to Him with the allure of love, enticing us up into the bedchamber where we will share the intimacies known only to lovers. Why should seduction only belong to the women of the night and to the world of sensual pleasure? Why should the Beloved only offer thorns and hardship? When the heart is called it opens to intimacy. When it is tenderly touched it melts. He who is love's master knows how to come "like a thief in the night" and whisper into the lover's ear what can never be told in daylight. Only He has the key to the heart of hearts, and when He wills He comes and blows on the spark He placed there before the dawn of creation.

Lovers learn to wait and to watch and to listen, because He who carries love's secrets comes in a guise that we least expect: "Whatever we think, He is the opposite of that." It is best to be bewildered and wondering, in a state of unknowing. In this condition of empty receptivity we can catch the thread of divine temptation:

> You thought union was a way
> you could decide to go.
> But the world of the soul follows
> things rejected and almost forgotten.
> Your true guide drinks
> from an undammed stream.[29]

The young men in the dream are able to follow love's call, even in the unexpected, lighthearted form it takes here, while the dreamer remains too identified with her preconditioned ideas about the path. She looks up and notices that the girls are having fun, but does not follow her guides unconditionally, because she does not expect love to appear in that form. She thinks she knows the way and turns into a narrow alley full of thorns, which is a traditional puritan picture of the spiritual path. In the patriarchal, Judeo-Christian tradition we are conditioned to resist temptation in all its forms, while the Sufi mystics have long recognized that love is a temptation not to be resisted. Love takes one beyond oneself, and thus beyond any idea one has of the path.

To be seduced by love is to be taken, entranced, away from oneself. Love's seduction is a feminine art which in our patriarchal culture carries the shadow of man's fear and desire. But the Beloved is not just a masculine god of justice and power, but also has a feminine side of mystery and beauty. He comes to us in unexpected ways, and both hides and reveals Himself, tempting us to come closer. We need to overcome our conditioning and allow ourself to be allured into love, to smell the sweet scent of His perfume and surrender ourself to the intoxication of an intangible embrace. This is the aspect of *jadhba* in which through love He frees our heart of anything except Himself.

He always remains hidden and the states of the lover's unknowingness deepen. "With the drawing of this Love and the voice of this Calling,"[30] we are seduced beyond the mind and the senses. Then the mystery of love's merging replaces the mystery of love's calling. Completely caught in the power of love, the lover becomes so lost the only outcome is annihilation.

The Beloved is so close to us, yet we cannot find Him. Through all our efforts we cannot reach Him. But through the feminine mystery of love He takes us beyond our own self to where He is:

> What you most want,
> what you travel around wishing to find,
> lose yourself as lovers lose themselves,
> and you'll *be* that.[31]

PRIMORDIAL NATURE

Each creature God made
Must live in its own true nature;
How could I resist my nature,
That lives for oneness with God?
Mechtild of Magdeburg[1]

THE SONG OF CREATION

"I was a Hidden Treasure. I longed to be known so I created the world." From the unknowable oneness were born the myriad wonders of the creation. What is visible reflects what is invisible. The creation in all its beauty and violence reflects the primordial oneness of the Creator. In His creation He makes Himself known to Himself: "None knows God but God." The purpose of creation is to reveal the Hidden Treasure that we call God. This purpose is held like a seed or embryo within every particle of creation. His longing to be known is the deepest force of nature.

Just as a sunflower follows the sun so does each particle of creation inwardly turn towards the Creator. Each particle unconsciously knows its Creator and thus embodies the purpose of its creation; in Henry Vaughan's words, "Each bush and oak doth know I AM."[2] This knowing is the innermost song of everything that is created. It is creation's song of praise to the Creator.

The song of creation is a song of praise. We hear it in the songbirds at dawn or see it in the first flowers opening in the spring. It is in our response to the beauty of a sunset or the glimpse of snow-capped mountains. At moments like these the heart opens in recognition of something we cannot name. For a moment the veils between the worlds lift and the beauty of this world awakens a memory of the inner beauty our heart knows but we have forgotten. We sense the song of praise that is in the spinning of every atom and in the motion of the stars. This praise is the imprint of His name in His creation. It is life's memory of its source. Dhû-l-Nûn experienced the creation's own song of praise:

> Whoever recollects God in reality, forgets all else beside Him, because all the creatures recollect Him, as is witnessed by those who experience a revelation. I experienced this state from evening prayer until one third of the night was over, and I heard the voices of the creatures in the praise of God, with elevated voices so that I feared for my mind. I heard the fishes who said, "Praised be the King, the Most Holy, the Lord."[3]

To praise Him is to witness that He is the Creator. The act of praise is the creation's recognition of the Creator. It was because He longed to be known that He created the world. In praising Him the creation tells the Creator that it knows Him. To praise Him is the esoteric, or hidden, purpose of creation, the most primal genetic print without which the universe would dissolve.

The act of praise is an act of remembrance that is the dynamic center of creation and yet mankind has forgotten this. We do not understand nature's deepest secret—"There is nothing that does not glorify Him in praise, *but you do not understand their glorification.*"[4] We have forgotten that everything remembers Him. We have forgotten that the act of praise does not have to be learnt but is an instinctual part of our very nature. The cells of our body praise Him, the neurons in our brain know Him, and yet this is held secret from us. We have to learn what all of creation constantly sings.

In becoming conscious, humanity lost touch with its instinctual knowledge of Him. Consciousness necessitates separation; it is consciousness that banished us from the paradisiacal state of unconscious oneness. Nature sings the song of oneness without the burden of consciousness. A stone, a flower, or an animal is itself and is in harmony with the whole, a wholeness that is not limited to the created world but also embraces the Creator. Nature unknowingly reflects the unmanifest, the Hidden Treasure, for "The world is no more than the Beloved's single face."[5]

We speak of the ecological oneness of nature, but there is a deeper oneness that nature embodies. The oneness of nature is a reflection of His oneness. Nature instinctively knows this inner, unmanifest wholeness just as a child instinctively knows its mother. But in nature this knowledge is not conscious. Consciousness is born with the pain of separation, with the banishment from paradise. With a child the birth of consciousness heralds the experience of separation from the mother, and the longing to return to paradise is often identified with the mother complex, the longing to return to the nurturing oneness of the mother. As consciousness grows so does the sense of our individuality, and the maturing of individual consciousness in adolescence is accompanied by the need to reject the parental world, in particular the world of the mother. Consciousness creates a drive to express individuality that is bound together with the need to separate. Without separation there can be no individuality, but the shadow side of this drive is the experience of isolation. The pain of consciousness is the pain of aloneness, and the more conscious we become the greater the sense of aloneness.

Consciousness carries the pain of separation from our own instinctual self, and with it the separation from our instinctual knowledge of the Creator. God walked in the Garden of Eden, but when Adam and Eve had eaten of the fruit of consciousness they hid themselves from Him and were then banished into the wilderness. This wilderness is life without the sense of oneness. When we feel cut off from nature or from our own instinctual self, it is this exile from a sense of oneness that haunts us.

In our contemporary society the sense of alienation from what is natural has reached an extreme. We place great value on self-expression and individuality but what appears more dominant is a collective feeling of isolation, futility, and meaninglessness. Both our inner cities and our inner selves carry the stamp of a collective desolation. Like an abandoned child we long for our mother, for life's nurture and sense of wholeness. Drugs have captivated us with their promise of paradise, the brief moment of ecstasy and forgetfulness. What our material culture cannot give us we seek in this shadowland of self-abuse. The pain of consciousness has the quality of a purposeless agony which we seek to escape through pleasure or addiction.

In the Company of Friends

CONSCIOUSNESS AND INDIVIDUALITY

The primal purpose of consciousness is to praise and to know Him. To this design, great temples and churches were built, rituals and music performed, sacred books written and studied. Until the advent of rationalism in the seventeenth century, the pursuit of knowledge had a spiritual foundation. Its underlying objective was to come to know the Creator and His creation more fully. In the last three centuries we have forgotten this heritage, and our materialistic culture and its companion greed have increasingly dominated the world. Consciousness has been enslaved by the desires of the ego and we have lost touch with its deeper spiritual purpose.

"I was a Hidden treasure and I longed to be known." He gave us the gift of consciousness so that we could come to know Him. What the world of nature knows unconsciously, humanity can know *consciously*. We cannot know His essence—"None knows God but God." But we can come to know His qualities, His names (*asmâ*) or attributes (*sifât*)). The sacred unveils Itself as we praise Him. If we take one step towards Him, He takes ten steps towards us. He longs to be known and He created within us the desire to know Him.

At the primordial covenant, when God asked the not-yet-created humanity, "Am I not your Lord?" humanity replied, "Yes, we witness it." He gave us consciousness so that we could witness Him. The affirmation that He is the Lord is the seed of consciousness. It is our primordial nature (*fitra*), our instinctual spiritual orientation. According to a famous *hadîth*, "Every child is born according to primordial nature; then his parents make him into a Jew, a Christian, or a

Zoroastrian."[6] Consciousness instinctively looks towards God, but because we have lost touch with our instinctual self we have lost touch with this natural orientation. We have identified consciousness with the ego and see the heights of consciousness in scientific achievements that give us power over our natural environment, or help our communication with each other. We have forgotten that the real purpose of consciousness is communion with God.

Witnessing Him we come to know Him, within ourself and within the world. The act of witnessing is essentially an individual act. Our individual consciousness witnesses Him. Even when we are praising God together with others, inwardly it is an individual act in which we acknowledge our own relationship to Him. In prayer and meditation we go within and offer the seed of our own uniqueness back to Him. We give our aloneness back to Him who is One and Alone. Spiritual life is in its essence a relationship of one to One, the individual and God. When Irina Tweedie told her teacher that she thought he could give her God, he laughed. Only He can reveal Himself in the heart of His servant, and "Allâh guides to His light whom He will."[7]

Just as the primal root of consciousness is the act of witnessing Him, so the root of individuality is the one-to-One relationship with God. We are made in His image. He who is One and Alone created that uniqueness within us, and when we fully acknowledge our uniqueness we acknowledge Him. Underlying our drive towards individuality is this spiritual drive. This is the motivating force behind our need to be different and to express our real nature. But in our culture we have identified the drive towards individuality solely with the ego and divorced this drive from its true purpose. This situation can only have negative results.

Consciousness is tremendously powerful, as can be seen in the power unleashed by our technological society. We are able to destroy our own planet, and some ecologists would argue that we have already achieved an irreversibly destructive situation. This dynamic of destruction is the ultimate result of separation. The ecological crisis is caused by our cultural separation from our natural environment, and it is highly symbolic that the splitting of the atom (the separation of the nucleus of a heavy atom into two smaller nuclei) created the atom bomb and released the possibility for ultimate physical destruction.[8]

Separation is a natural movement away from the center, but there comes a critical moment when the center loses its cohesive hold and the process becomes destructive. When a system is no longer held together at its core it falls apart. Our solar system is held in place by the gravitational pull of the sun, without which the individual planets would spin off into the universe. Civilizations are also held together, by values, ideals, or great leaders. History is littered with the ruins of civilizations which have fallen apart as their center, their ideals, degenerated. This is true of the present time. Addicted by the desires of the ego and without any cohesive non-ego values, we are surrounded by experiences of disintegration, as Yeats expresses in ominous imagery:

> Turning and turning in the widening gyre
> The falcon cannot hear the falconer;
> Things fall apart; the center cannot hold;
> Mere anarchy is loosed upon the world.[9]

"The falcon cannot hear the falconer." We are so buried in materialism that we can no longer hear the call of the center. The muezzin who calls us to prayer from within our own souls speaks a language so primitive that we cannot understand it. Meister Eckhart describes God as "the sigh in the soul," but this cry is so different from the demands of our sophisticated world that even when we hear it we do not know what it means or how to respond. The path of separation has taken us so far from our natural center that we have forgotten the purpose of our journey.

The purpose of separation is to offer what is unique and individual back to the Great Artist who created no two things alike. Nature does this each moment. Each leaf, each raindrop, each created thing glorifies Him just through being itself:

> As kingfishers catch fire, dragonflies draw flame;
> As tumbled over rim in roundy wells
> Stones ring; like each tucked string tells, each hung bell's
> Bow sung finds tongue to fling out broad its name;
> Each mortal thing does one thing and the same:
> Deals out being indoors each one dwells;
> Selves—goes itself; *myself* it speaks and spells,
> Crying *What I do is me for that I came.*[10]

He made us unique so that through us He could come to know His own uniqueness. The natural world lives this spiritual truth by being itself. It cannot be other. In a dream a friend had a conversation with a fox in which he asked the fox if it would always be cunning and sly. The fox replied, "A fox will be what a fox is." The natural world unknowingly fulfills its deepest purpose and is an example for humanity. The need that people today often feel to reconnect with nature has at its core the need to reawaken this instinctual spiritual attitude. It is not just the beauty and peace of nature that attract us, but an inner awareness that nature lives its deepest purpose, which we have forgotten. This is the most primal nourishment we seek. This is the manna we crave in our urban wasteland.

Nostalgically we may long to return to the land, or reconnect with cultures that lived in spiritual harmony with the outer and inner world. But this is not a real answer to our problems, and nostalgia is often just an activation of the mother complex, a longing to return to a nurturing forgetfulness, to return to the warmth of the collective and not have to suffer the pain of isolation. The path of separation has a purpose that can only be fulfilled through individuality. We need to return *within our individual self* to the primal roots of our being, and there rediscover the spiritual connection we have lost, realize the spiritual purpose of our drive towards individuality, which is to offer our own uniqueness back to Him. Then the circle will be complete. From the path of separation we will walk to the road to union.

HE WHO KNOWS HIMSELF

From the perspective of the ego the goal of individuality is self-determination: the freedom to do what you want. This is the ideal of our present society, yet in fact it is an imprisonment within the limited horizons of the ego, because it is the ego that generates our desires. Furthermore, because the essence of the ego is its sense of separation, if we give ourself to its desires we will only experience separation, which leads to isolation and alienation. In contrast, from a spiritual perspective individuality is a gateway to the infinite, as Yeats simply expressed: "The love of God is infinite for every human soul because every human soul is unique, no other can satisfy the same need in God." To realize our individuality is to realize His uniqueness. We are made in the image of God and to know ourself is to know Him, as in the famous *hadîth*, "He who knows himself knows his Lord."

To know ourself we have to go within and face the darkness that separates what we really are from what we like to think we are. We have to confront and accept the rejected, unacknowledged parts of ourself, what Jung termed "the shadow." Our true nature is covered by conditioning, our individual self repressed in favor of how we were told to be by our parents and our environment. In our "civilized" culture it is our natural, instinctual self that is most deeply buried and covered with the wounds of rejection. But if we consciously accept this "dark beast" we will find that it contains the secret of our natural relationship to God. At its deepest level our primordial nature is a state of communion, the prayer of our innermost being.

We are born into this world to praise Him. The instinct to worship and the instinct to survive are the only two instincts with which we are born. Everything else is developed later. To praise Him is to realize the sacred nature of our individuality. Prayer is not something learnt, but the natural orientation of our very being. Prayer *is* our true self expressing itself and through this self-expression becoming conscious of its divine nature:

> The Divine Being needs His faithful in order
> to manifest Himself; reciprocally the faithful
> needs the Divine Being in order to be invested

with existence. In this sense, his Prayer is his very being, his very capacity for being; it is the being of his hexeity demanding full realization; and this prayer implies its fulfillment since it is nothing other than the desire expressed by the Godhead still hidden in the solitude of His unknowingness: "I was a Hidden Treasure, I yearned to be known."[11]

Without prayer we would be bound within the imprisoning walls of the ego, unaware of our eternal self. Through the act of prayer we give birth to Him within our own self; the unknowable God which is pure non-being, beyond existence, becomes incarnated as a personal God who is the object of our devotions. "I give Him also life by knowing Him in my heart."[12]

SEPARATION FROM THE COLLECTIVE

Prayer or praise is the natural expression of our being. In prayer our divine individuality is acknowledged and made conscious. Consciousness which has brought us the pain of separation and the anguish of aloneness now fulfills its purpose in witnessing Him, and we experience this state of fulfillment. In our uniqueness we come to know His uniqueness. Through our relationship to His uniqueness we come to know the real nature of our uniqueness. This is the return of the exile, who has come to know himself and His Lord:

"O soul at peace, return unto thy Lord,
well-pleased, well-pleasing!
Enter thou among my servants
Enter thou My Paradise!"[13]

But this return to paradise, this awakening of a natural state of prayer, is bought at a price. Just as the initial awakening of consciousness brought about the pain of separation, so does this return journey involve further pain of separation: separation from the collective.

It was consciousness that separated us from the instinctual oneness of life, from the unknowing state of wholeness. Yet we did not make this journey in isolation but as a part of the human race. As the child grows into consciousness it is held within the arms of the collective. The sense of aloneness that consciousness evokes is countered by the support of the collective. This is very evident in adolescence in the conflicting drives to be alone and to be a part of a peer group. A gang offers the collective support that contains the pain of individuality.

In tribal societies the transition into adult consciousness was marked by an initiation that separated the individual from the world of childhood. Women are naturally initiated by menstruation and then the pain of childbirth. Male initiation is often by circumcision, a painful ritual that takes boys out of the maternal circle into the male world. In both instances the separation from childhood into the consciousness and responsibility of being an adult is usually accompanied by a period of ritual seclusion before the adolescent is welcomed into the adult group. Separation, pain, and isolation are part of the transition into the adult collective world. In our present-day society we have lost much of the formalized ritual to help us through this period, although gang initiations are a shadow dynamic that fulfill some of these patterns.

However, in whatever culture we live, adolescence is a transition into a greater individual consciousness in which we are supported by the collective. We become a member of a collective social group which has its own values. Instinctively we "fit in" and adopt these new patterns of conditioning, which may offer a greater sense of individual freedom than childhood, but also delineate our patterns of behavior and inner attitudes. Even the "rebel" is attracted to belong to a counterculture, which again gives the individual self the support of a collective identity. True individuality demands a degree of separation that most find too painful to tolerate.

THE JOURNEY TO THE SOURCE

But the evolution of consciousness need not stop at the passage into the adult collective. There are those who are driven by an inner need to take the path of individuation, of discovering an individual self that is not determined by collective conditioning. This is a lonely path that takes us inward, away from the collective. In our Western society it means going beyond the materialistic and ego-oriented values that dominate our collective consciousness, and discovering that our real individuality does not belong to the ego, but to something more ancient and sacred: our primordial nature.

The following dream describes the journey beyond the collective towards a natural state of prayer. It is a journey which involves the "risk" of transgressing collective values:

> I am in a jungle setting of rolling hills with mountain areas on many sides. There is a river, large enough for small merchant-ship traffic.

The river is almost always out of sight but is very present throughout the dream. I am a professional of some kind (possibly an airline pilot or an attorney) and have come to make a trek up-country along the river. There is a risk involved, and I seem to have left a good life and good friends and family behind to be in this place.

The jungle is full of "natives," who are not all visible because of the terrain. They seem attuned to the natural, spiritual flow of the place, but they must be wary because of the prevailing "colonial" type of authority. None of the "authority" people are visible in the dream but their presence is felt.

The natives move across the terrain in a kind of stealthy dance, and I am involved in following this movement as I work my way upriver. Word is out that the authorities are active in suppressing native activity and have just killed two persons who were engaged in "illegal" activity on the river, and cut out their hearts. The natives are carrying these hearts in a small container, which they pass along as they move through the jungle.

I am suddenly aware of a pinpoint of red light high on one of the mountains, and I see a corresponding spot of light on a rock near me. It is as if a laser beam passes between the two points. As I examine this I realize that there are a few natives near me who are involved with other connections to the red light source high on the mountain. There is a spiritual quality about their attention. They sit facing in the general direction of the light, and I am aware of more and more who are involved. All seem to be quietly chanting, and I can hear their sound throughout the landscape. The sense of risk has prevailed throughout the dream and continues now. I join in the movement, sitting on the ground where I first saw the spot of light on the rock. There is a sense of awe, spirituality, and tension.

The jungle symbolizes the primal, instinctual world through which the river of life winds back to its source. It is this jungle that civilization has attempted to cultivate and colonize; the tree-cutting rape of the great rain forests of the world tragically images our cultural attitude towards our natural inner self. Utilitarianism and greed have desecrated the sacred groves of the psyche as our society places material possession above any inner values.

But the inner world is as endless as space, and although we may have "colonized" aspects of our natural self, if we are prepared to risk the journey beyond the known boundaries of consciousness we can still discover an unpolluted inner life. It is this urge that draws the dreamer upstream, into the hinterland of his own self. He describes his dream-ego as an airline pilot or attorney, both contemporary figures dominated by the ideals of masculine, rational consciousness. They personify our Western collective values. This is the world the dreamer will have to leave behind and he feels the "risk involved" in leaving behind this familiar and established identity, these collective values of "the good life."

The collective provides the security of belonging, while the inner journey confronts us with the uncertainty of self-discovery. To venture into the inner jungle, to go upstream towards our own inner nature, means leaving behind "a good life and good friends and family." All those who have travelled the inner path know this feeling, and when this dream was shared within our group this image of departure evoked sympathy and understanding. The loneliness of the journey is a price paid by every traveller, because in order to discover our true self we need to leave behind the comforts and familiarity of the collective that actually imprison us.

The inhabitants of this inner world are very different from the professional world the dreamer has left. The "natives" are "attuned to the natural, spiritual flow of the place." It is in the unconscious that we find our natural spirituality which has been banished by scientific materialism. Spirituality is not something that we have to learn, but have to rediscover. If we dare to be drawn inward we can find our own instinctual attunement, where we are in harmony with life's spiritual flow. Deep within us there is no separation between life and spirit, but the greater the conditioning, the stronger the influence of rationalism and materialism, the deeper we may need to go to discover this spiritual attunement. These cultural values are the "colonial" powers which have dominated consciousness and pressed their authority on our unconscious through the pervasive influence of the collective conditioning.

The natives are understandably wary of these "invisible authorities" because the collective will try to resist any attempt to undermine its influence. Psychological conditioning is not like pieces of furniture that can be moved or avoided, but is made up of psychic forces that have gained power and autonomy. They are more like members of the family who have established patterns of relationships and behavior, and do not like their values to be challenged, their patterns to be upset. On the path of individuation Christ's words ring poignantly: "And a man's foes shall be they of his own household."[14]

ESCAPING THE COLLECTIVE

Often an individual feels the urge to challenge the collective, to actively condemn the accepted social values. On the inner journey this is rarely advisable. To confront the collective psyche, either through an outer action or an inner confrontational attitude, is to evoke the dynamic of persecution and the scapegoat archetype.[15] It is only too easy to end up playing either the antagonist or the victim and using all one's valuable energy attacking or defending one's inner position against the overwhelming power of the collective. Then rather than going deeper within, one is caught in the constellated opposites of the individual and the collective.

This constellation of opposites can appear fulfilling. Some people are naturally attracted to being victims, while others enjoy the excitement of playing the hero, the individual against the mass. But both attitudes are frequently an egotistic inflation, playing the victim being often a negative inflation (when everybody is against you, you are also the center of attention). Jung was very aware of the dangers of the heroic attitude. When he had a dream about shooting Siegfried, the mythic German hero, his inner voice insisted that he understand the dream at once. He realized that Siegfried was an attitude of will, of imposing one's views upon others. He understood that "this identity and my heroic idealism had to be abandoned, for there are higher things than the ego's will, and to these one must bow."[16] The goal of the inner journey is not to change the collective but to change oneself.

The easiest way to free oneself from the grip of the collective is through disengagement and detachment, rather than confrontation or criticism. If other people feel that what is most important is acquiring a new house or a new car, maybe that is a necessary experience for them. Judgment or criticism detracts attention and energy from the inner journey. In order to focus within ourself and discover our real individual nature we need to disengage and become detached from others. Criticism, like confrontation, is a form of psychological entanglement in which we can easily give our energy to a shadow dynamic.

"You come naked into the world and you go naked. When you come to a spiritual teacher you have to be naked."[17] The values and conditioning that we have acquired from the collective are not our real nature. For example, we were not born with a possessive materialistic nature. Many "primitive" tribes do not have the notion of personal ownership. This is true of some of the hill tribes of New Guinea, and I experienced the sad effect of Western values when I was working with them on a Australian-owned coconut plantation. Often the first purchase that these Highlanders made with their new money was a box with a lock.

Another Western disease is to be continually thinking and planning for the future. While children live in the present moment, as adults we are conditioned into thinking of the future. "What are you going to do when you grow up?" is a question that begins to pressure children in a way antithetical to the spontaneity of their real nature. On the spiritual path we need to regain this spontaneity and live in the present: "If you think of the future and make plans, you don't trust in God. Never think of tomorrow ... Only the moment of now matters."[18]

Our conditioned attitude towards the future was portrayed in a friend's dream in which she left the world of the white men and made a dangerous journey to join a group of Native Americans. She found that the natives had converted a bank building into a community center, illustrating a radically different set of values, in which being part of a community or group offers the security we are conditioned to believe is found in a bank. Written in large letters on this bank was a humorously ungrammatical statement, "WHITE MAN SAVES STRANGE FOR FUTURE."

What is acquired can be discarded. We need not be the slaves of the collective, and as we glimpse behind the veils of the outer world we sense different values which are far more precious. These are the values of the Self and the feeling of real freedom that can only come from detachment.

But the pull of the collective is very powerful. The collective thought-forms and attitudes of millions of people have a tremendous effect. To disengage and remain free is a difficult work, and only too often we unknowingly slip back, or are overwhelmed by doubts or feelings of anxiety. Are we really right to dismiss the striving for material security or are we just deluding ourself with illusory dreams? At these times the support of a spiritual group is invaluable, for it provides a protection against the collective. The energy generated by the group reinforces our inner convictions and supports our quest to find what is real. And because a Sufi group values the individual rather than any collective attitude, it does not just replace one set of collective values with another (as often happens in groups or sects). Rather it provides a sacred space in which we can discover our true self, our own individual relationship with the Beyond.

Not only is there the outer group but also the spiritual tradition that helps us in the journey beyond the collective. We feel how we are treading a path that has been trod by countless others, each solitary pilgrim walking away from the outer world and from the collective, towards Him who is our innermost being. "Solitary, God loves only the solitary,"[19] and on the journey to Him we must be alone. Yet in our aloneness we are supported and encouraged by all those who have walked before us. We are in the invisible company of the friends of God.

The energy and presence of the tradition are always inwardly there for those who follow a particular path. But the tradition is often more accessible at the group meetings. We are aware that wayfarers have met together in meditation for centuries, silently going within to the heart of hearts where the Beloved is waiting. In our togetherness we value our aloneness, we feel the bond of those who "love one another for God's sake."

THE ILLEGAL ACTIVITIES OF LOVE

In the dream of the journey through the jungle the dreamer begins to become attuned to the dance of the natives, and it is with this natural spiritual movement that he makes his way upriver. This dance is the natural rhythm of the soul, in which we learn to live in harmony with our deepest being. This is the dance of primitive rituals and also the joyous clapping of an infant's hands. It is the joyous dance of creation, the eternal "yes" that sings in the blood, without which there would be no blossom on the trees or light in a lover's eyes.

This dance is a state of prayer, a natural way of being in which we praise Him, but it has been outlawed by a masculine culture striving to dominate nature. When the Puritans banned the maypole dances because of their hedonistic, erotic qualities, our culture repressed the earth's sacred dance in which fertility and praise belong together. We are born in order to praise Him, and in this act we are not separate from the rest of His creation. Within everything that is manifest, His song of love can be heard.

The dance of the natives in this dream is the soul's celebration of its divinity, the devotee's response to the heart's call to prayer. But the "authorities" are active in "suppressing" this "activity" and two natives have had their hearts cut out. The heart is our spiritual center, the home of the Self, the abode of "that Person in the heart, no bigger than a thumb, maker of past and future."[20] Without a heart there can be no connection with our eternal nature, no feeling of the infinite. By "cutting out the heart" the authorities of the collective have denied us access to our innermost being, they have locked the door of love that opens into His presence.

This action poignantly symbolizes the collective's desire to imprison us in the temporal world. The mind and the ego can be conditioned, as the advertising media exploit to its fullest impact, but the heart cannot be collectively controlled. While the mind often expresses thoughts programmed by outside influences, the heart is its own master, and often surprises us with unexpected feelings.

The heart contains the organ of our spiritual consciousness and the Self is its guardian. In the innermost chamber of the heart there is a place that no human being can reach, not even one whom we love. The mind and the ego cannot disturb this space, or influence it with any desire. It belongs only to Him, as the ninth-century Sufi, al-Hakîm at-Tirmidhî, describes:

> God placed the heart within the cavity of the human chest, and it belongs to God alone. No one can have any claim to it. God holds the heart between two of His fingers, and no one is allowed access to it: neither an angel nor a prophet; no created being in the whole creation. God alone TURNS it as He wishes. Within the heart God placed the knowledge of Him and He lit it with the Divine Light.... By this light He gave the heart eyes to see.[21]

Here, in the heart of hearts, we are in a constant state of prayer. If the door to the heart is closed, we lose contact with this state of communion.

In our extrovert culture the spiritual ways of the heart have been forgotten. Love's intimacy has come to refer only to sexual passion, and the idea of a divine lover is found only in myth or the fantasies of romance novels. A friend dreamed that she was living in her parents' house and her lover came and rang on the doorbell, bearing a bouquet of flowers. She opened the door and invited him in, but there was nowhere that they could be alone together. Her inner lover had come to her with the gifts of love, with symbols of her spiritual flowering. But in order to be alone with her heart's desire and experience the tenderness of His touch, she needs to leave the house of her conditioning, where there is no room for such intimacy. The heart's longing needs a space of seclusion, a place for spiritual communion to unfold.

We each need to find an inner space where we are not disturbed by social values that tell us that we should be doing something practical and that the heart's vulnerability will lead only to pain. Opening to love we open to the pain of love as much as to its bliss, but that is the price of being His lover. We give ourself to a love that does not belong to the world, to a longing that will take us to our real home.

Together as a group we create the conditions for finding our own inner space. The group commitment to the path forms a wall around the garden of our soul, allowing us to be inwardly open and yet protected from the antagonistic influences of the collective. In our meditation we go within the heart and surrender the mind and the ego to love. We are awakened to our primal state of union, a moment that is eternally present within the heart, because it is the heart's natural state of being. In the innermost chamber of the heart we are with Him, and as we meditate this state of union filters into consciousness. In meditation we give ourself to our unique relationship with Him, the one-to-One relationship of lover and Beloved, and so we transcend the boundaries of the collective. Within the heart we are free because we belong to Him. This is the paradox of spiritual freedom, which the ego cannot grasp. To be free is to be bound in love to Him.

LIGHT UPON LIGHT

In the final part of the dream about the journey to the source the dreamer becomes aware of a red pinpoint of light high in the mountains, and of a corresponding point of light on a rock near him. The two spots of light are connected as if by a laser beam. The natives around him also have their own connection to the red light in the mountains, and they sit facing in the direction of the light. It is of great significance that the natives and the dreamer *each have their own connection.* This stresses the individuality of our relationship with the source.

The light on the rock beside the dreamer is the light of the Self which connects with His light high in the mountains. Through the fire of our longing the light within the heart rises to meet His light and His light comes to meet us. This is the secret of the mystical communion, the journey of the soul back to the source, as the thirteenth-century Sufi, Najm al-Dîn Kubrâ, describes:

> There are lights which ascend and lights which descend. The ascending lights are the lights of the heart; the descending lights are those of the Throne. The lower-self [the ego] is the veil between the Throne and the heart. When this veil is rent and a door opens in the heart, like springs towards like. Light rises toward light and light comes down upon light, "and it is light upon light." (Qur'an 24:35)....
>
> Each time the heart sighs for the Throne, the Throne sighs for the heart, so they come to meet ... Each time a light rises up from you, a

> light comes down towards you, and each time a
> flame rises from you a corresponding flame
> comes down towards you.... If their energies
> are equal, they meet half-way.... But when the
> substance of light has grown in you, then this
> becomes a Whole in relation to what is of the
> same nature in heaven: then it is the substance
> of light in Heaven which yearns for you and is
> attracted to your light, and it descends towards
> you. This is the secret of the mystical journey....[22]

When the Beloved looks towards His servant the spark
in the heart is kindled and this light seeks its source.
The light in the heart seeking its source creates the
feeling of longing, and this longing in turn attracts His
light. The greater the longing burns within the lover the
more it attracts the attention of the Beloved: "each time
the heart sighs for the Throne, the throne sighs for the
heart, so that they come to meet ..." This is the secret
of the heart's sorrow, and why longing is the golden
thread that takes us home. Within the heart of His
servant He calls to Himself, and He answers His own
call: "I respond to the call of the caller when he calls
to me."[23]

The heart of the lover belongs to his Beloved, and
it is within the heart that the mystery of union is
conceived and born. The light from above and the light
from below meet and in this meeting He reveals
Himself to Himself. He gives birth to Himself, as Rûmî
expresses: "Sorrow for His sake is a treasure in my
heart. My heart is *Light upon light*, a beautiful Mary
with Jesus in the womb."[24]

The flame of longing that burns within the lover is
His light in the world. This flame polishes the mirror of
the heart until He can see His own face in the heart of

His servant. This polishing is the inner work and the pain of the path which wear away the lover until only the Beloved remains.

The work of the lover is to stay true to the longing and remain focused on the source. In a dream a friend asked her Beloved what she could do for Him, and He simply replied, "Be there for Me." If we remain inwardly attentive to the needs of the heart we attune our whole being to His purpose, to love's unfolding. This attention is a natural state of prayer because we are doing what our own heart desires. It is not imposed upon us by any outside influence. Rather it is consciousness following the call of the heart rather than the desires of the ego.

Najm al-Dîn Kubrâ explains that the "lower-self," the ego, is the veil between the Throne and the heart. This veil is "rent" when we seek a deeper fulfillment than the ego can offer, and stay true to this seeking. Then the mystery of *light upon light* begins, a process so different from the ego's drive for self-gratification that this inner dynamic cannot be understood by the rational mind. The heart knows but the mind is increasingly left in a state of confusion. We leave behind the logic of the world of duality and enter into a reality that can only be explained by the language of merging and union.

The light within the heart of the wayfarer is nourished by His light and grows until it is the same as the light from above, for "as above so below." The light above and the light below merge in a state of oneness in which the soul is united and yet unique, is absorbed and also its own individual self. In the state of absorption the part returns to the whole and is both lost and found. Separation is banished and yet the individual nature of what is created remains. Our uniqueness is realized as a part of the whole, as a woman glimpsed in the following dream:

> In that place of not being awake and not being asleep, I heard a chorus of women's voices and I had the impression of women in the sky who were coming in a V-formation, and they were singing the most heavenly music—it was incredible, beautiful. And then one of these women did a virtuoso, it was as if her voice soared out from the rest of the chorus. And if you've ever heard a bird give its all to a song with incredible trills and swelling of the chest, that's what this woman did. I remember lying there and hearing her voice and the range was incredible. She would swoop down and reach its lowest note and then soar up....

As the dreamer awoke she realized that the singer was herself, and the song was her own self in praise. This is the same glorification as Mary's, "My soul doth magnify the Lord,"[25] when she gave thanks that His child was conceived within her. He calls us to Him and then gives birth to Himself within our heart and what is born is our own primordial state of prayer and praise.

The creation mirrors the Creator, and in the heart of His servant this act is made conscious. This consciousness is an act of witnessing that He is the Lord. The consciousness of the Self is a state of prayer in which His uniqueness is mirrored in our uniqueness.

> I am He whom I love, and He whom I love is I.
> We are two spirits dwelling in one body.
> If thou seest me, thou seest Him;
> And if thou seest Him, thou seest us both.[26]

Spiritual life is a state of oneness *and* duality. In meditation we merge into the heart and are lost in oneness. In waking consciousness we live in His world of duality which within the heart we *know* to be one. We love the world because it is a reflection of Him, and yet we long to be back united with Him. We surrender to the pain of separation because only then can we offer Him our prayers and praise. We long for Him when we are separate from Him, and in our longing the painful bond of love draws us closer to Him. Through surrender we free ourself from the ego and its chains of separation, and yet He desires that we experience separation:

> I want union with Him, and He wants separation;
> Thus I leave what I want so that His wish comes true.[27]

To be conscious of the pain of separation is to know the state of union. The light within the heart is the consciousness of the heart, the consciousness of the Self. He wished the Self to experience separation so that it might know Him. In our longing and prayer His hidden treasure is revealed, His longing to be known is made conscious: "light rises towards light and light comes down upon light, 'and it is light upon light.'" *Light upon light* is His revelation to Himself, and His greatest gift is for His lover to participate in this revelation. Through the hearts of His servants He comes closer to Himself.

A STATE OF BEING

The journey to the source is a journey to the center of one's being where the heart is connected directly to

Him. This center is the rock of the Self, undisturbed by the influence of the outer world, by conditioning or collective attitudes. Sitting on the ground near to this spot within himself, the dreamer feels "a sense of awe, spirituality, and tension." He has made the journey to this place of inner connectedness and senses the numinousity of the sacred ground of his innermost self. Here he will discover the nature of his own communion with the beyond, with the "light source high on the mountain."

Spiritual life is a state of being, a natural state of being with oneself and with God. Because it is a state of being we can never find it, but through our searching we tear away the veils that separate us from this consciousness of the heart. What we discover is that we know how to be with God. A familiarity and awe, an intimacy and distance are woven into the substance of the soul. Each of us will experience and express this state of being in our own way, for "Every being has his own appropriate mode of prayer and glorification."[28]

Within us we discover the way the Beloved wishes us to be with Him, and then we allow this state of being into our life. In our individual way we mirror His uniqueness. Rûmî tells the story of Moses, who overhears a shepherd praying:

> "God,
> where are You? I want to help You, to fix Your shoes
> and comb Your hair. I want to wash Your clothes
> and pick the lice off. I want to bring You milk,
> to kiss Your little hands and feet when it's time
> for You to go to bed. I want to sweep Your room
> and keep it neat. God, my sheep and goats
> are Yours. All I can say, remembering You,
> is ayyyy and ahhhhhhh."

Moses, affronted by the shepherd's natural intimacy with God and way of addressing Him with such everyday language, criticizes the poor shepherd, who tears his clothes, sighs, and wanders into the desert. But then God comes to Moses, and says:

> *You have separated me*
> *from one of my own. Did you come as a Prophet to*
> *unite, or to sever?*
> *I have given each being a separate and unique way*
> *of seeing and knowing and saying that knowledge.*
> *What seems wrong to you is right for him.*
> *What is poison to one is honey to someone else.*[29]

Each in our own way we learn to love Him, to give ourself in love to Him. The gestures of lovers are intimate and individual. As God says to Moses, what matters is not the form of expression, but what is within, the attitude of the lover, the fire in the heart: "*Forget phraseology, I want burning,* burning."

After God has spoken, Moses runs after the shepherd and, finally catching up with him, says, "I was wrong.

> God has revealed to me
> that there are no rules for worship.
> Say whatever
> and however your loving tells you to."

But the shepherd in his loving has gone beyond any form and he thanks Moses,

> "You applied the whip and my horse shied and jumped out of itself. The Divine Nature and my human nature came together...."

The return journey takes us through the world of forms into the formlessness of His presence. Through our acts of devotion, our longing and perseverance, our own individual nature is melted and then He merges into us. This is one of the greatest mysteries. The Beloved merges into the lover, the ocean flows into the dewdrop.

When the door of the heart is opened His infinite emptiness enters. What remains of His servant becomes a shell. Everything else is burnt away, dissolved in the currents of His love. The more our attention is with God, the more we are made empty for His sake. The deepest prayer is without words. The most primal praise is silence, a silence in which the very being of the lover is increasingly absorbed somewhere, far beyond the mind and the senses.[30] The Beloved needs us to make known to Himself His own non-being, His essential emptiness. We are made empty because He is empty. In our emptiness we bring this hidden treasure into the world.

THE SCIENCE OF LOVE

All this talk and turmoil and noise and movement is
outside the veil;
inside the veil is silence and calm and peace.
Bâyezîd Bistâmî[1]

THE PURPOSE OF OUR PROBLEMS

The heart holds so many contradictions. We experience pain and joy, loneliness and love. Walking the path of the heart we are thrown into these contradictions, into the pain of our love, into the bliss of our longing. So often we are confused; we feel lost and helpless. Somewhere there is a thread that guides us, a hand that holds us, but it is hidden under the confusion and chaos of our personalities and problems. How can we stay true to the real purpose of love and not become distracted? How can we walk this narrowest of paths and not become lost in the contortions of the mind and the maze of the psyche?

There is a science to love, to the way the hidden core of the heart opens. Our problems, even the difficulties that seem insurmountable, have a practical purpose. Jung writes that the most serious problems in life are never fully solved. Through working on them we are preserved from inertia, from "stultification and petrification."[2] The conflict created by our problems provides the friction that wears away the ego. Because the major problems are fundamentally insoluble, they point beyond the ego to deeper levels of our being. Although we cannot solve these problems we can grow out of them.[3] We can grow into a dimension of ourself where they no longer hold us in their grip.

Underlying all our difficulties and our desire to resolve them is the longing for an inner state of unity in which there are no conflicts or distortions. We are driven by this inner sense of wholeness, a memory of perfection, which does not let us accept the limitations of our difficulties. But the ego cannot experience wholeness. The nature of the ego is separation. Only if we "grow out" of the ego can we reach the unity of the Self. Yet the ego cannot go beyond itself, just as the mind cannot go beyond the mind. The impossibility of reaching wholeness evokes the deepest despair.

On the path of love we are constantly confronted with the primal problem of humanity, that we are separate from Him whom we love. We long for the clear light of the Self, the sunshine of the soul which we remember. In the innermost core of our being there is only love, an outflowing of tenderness, an embrace of eternity. But as we lie awake our tears tell another story, of the pain of being born, of the sorrow of souls that are separate. These tears melt the heart and cleanse us. Their despair drives us forward.

This path we tread has been trod for centuries. So many wayfarers have walked barefoot in the dust of the world, facing the distortions of their true nature, confronting the impossibility of reaching any haven. We all share the one pain of separation, and yet for each of us this pain is personal and unique. It bleeds us in the most difficult places of our personal life and intimate self. Each in our own way we learn to endure and then to surrender; we each need to come to our own realization that only He can help us, and that all our struggle is of no avail. This surrender is the step out of the ego, without which there can be no progress but only an endless turning on the wheel of suffering. Every spiritual path takes the seeker to the place of no return, where we have to embrace the situation that hurts us most.

Along this ancient road we are taken one by one, crying our own tears, feeling the terrible futility of our own efforts. To surrender is to accept what has been given and not to ask that it be otherwise; and yet this contradicts every human desire to change and improve our situation. To accept the pain, the difficulty, the despair goes against our nature, our need to struggle.

What will become of us if we want nothing? What will happen if we accept our limitations, the difficulties of our own personal situations? When we cease to struggle, to gasp for freedom, will we be drowned by these problems? Or will something else take over? Will a fragrance from a different dimension enter our lives?

If we look carefully within us we will each find that there is a fundamental pain or problem that is insoluble. However hard we try, it cannot be resolved. We cannot conquer it with our will, or untangle it with all our concentration. It is somehow as solid as the very foundation of our self. This painful problem is the lock that binds us to this world, to matter and the meaning of our incarnation. It has a purpose beyond the pain, beyond the story that it tells, beyond anything we might think. It has a purpose so simple that in our search for truth it is easily overlooked. It says that we are human and in being human we have limitations and faults.

We need to know the nature of our limitation, and the more we search for God, for Truth, the more we need to be reminded that we are not That. We cry for Him. We long to get closer to Him, to merge into His infinite freedom and bliss. But we are unable. We are caught here in the web of our self, in the prison of our own inadequacy. This is the tremendous paradox of the path. The closer we come to Him the more we know the nature of our own limitations, and that we will always be separate.

Love has a science that turns the human heart back to God. Giving ourself to God we give ourself to a process that is as simple as love itself. This world is the stage on which our spiritual self is reborn. What the ego regards as an impossible problem is in reality the place where matter and spirit are bonded together. It is the place where His grace is most bountiful. He who is without limitation allows Himself to experience limitation through us. In surrendering to the experience we offer it back to Him. If we resist, if we seek to avoid or reject the situation, we stand between Him and the experience. Then the ego blocks the flow of grace, and we are left with nothing but pain.

Everything within us cries out to avoid the problem that is our own personal crucifixion. Every cell of the body, every pulse of the psyche, is appalled at the idea of acceptance. It means denying the power and autonomy of the ego, and accepting our position as servant. We are where we need to be at each moment. Limitation is the very nature of the ego and cannot be resolved by changing our situation. The potency of despair is realized through the acceptance of our limitation. Only through the touch of Him who is without limits can we experience freedom. It is His gift that He gives to those who know that He is Lord.

THE RELIABLE LOOP

The journey home is a marathon of endurance and acceptance. This is no frivolous undertaking, because the depths of pain and despair can appear endless. Gerard Manley Hopkins describes the overwhelming intensity of what we find within us:

> O the mind, mind has mountains; cliffs of fall
> Frightful, sheer, no-man-fathomed. Hold them cheap
> May who ne'er hung there. Nor does long our small
> Durance deal with that steep or deep.[4]

To hang on in the abyss of our self requires every effort. Sometimes it seems as if there is nothing to hold on to, and yet in the midst of all our difficulties hangs the thin thread of our devotion and trust. The Sufis call this the "reliable loop" (*al-'urwa al-wathqâ*), and without it we would be lost in the whirlpool of the psyche. For one friend it appeared as a golden ring which he could inwardly hold on to whenever he was confronted by despair. The "reliable loop" comes from above and is imprinted into our soul. It is a direct connection to the Self and gives us something to hold on to that is not contaminated by our psychological problems. It is always present within us, though it is easily hidden by doubts and desires.

The "reliable loop" does not present a resolution to our problems. Rather it offers a point of stability and inner reassurance. It enables the wayfarer to walk across the water of his inner chaos. This "reliable loop" is a bond of grace that is given to those who seek Him, allowing them to "hold on in spite of everything." The more difficult our problems, the greater the danger of being submerged beneath them, the more important is the circle of trust, this imprint of the path.

Our problems can force us to find this inner security, to bring into consciousness the golden loop or thread. But this only happens if we seek after something beyond the ego. If we look for a resolution on the level of the ego, if we run away from the pain, then the loop of trust remains hidden. We have to make the step out of ourself in order to align ourself with the grace that is found on the path. In the words of Abû Sa'îd ibn Abî-l-Khayr:

> Take one step
> away from yourself and—
> behold!—the Path!

This path is often most visible in the company of friends. Because we come together for His sake we are inwardly reminded of our innermost trust and faith. It is an invisible presence in the air, a fragrance that we sense around us. This is the security of a Sufi group: being together we remind each other of what can be found within the heart. We are awakened to the certainty of the Self.

Yet at the same time the energy of the group may itself evoke pain and suffering. The purpose of the path is to transcend the ego, and this process, experienced in the group, can easily activate difficulties and problems. Often when people first come they will have a dream which outlines the work that needs to be undertaken, the pain that needs to be confronted. One person had a dream after her first visit in which she angers a Mexican woman. The Mexican woman arranges to have the dreamer killed by sticking needles above her eyes. In the final part of the dream the dreamer experiences the needles penetrating her, though instead of death she experiences what she describes as "heavy ecstasy," an ecstasy in which the whole body is included.

The dreamer felt that the Mexican woman imaged her own natural, instinctual feminine self, which she had angered through rejection. Like many women she had been conditioned to overvalue the masculine, and if she began to abandon her conditioning she would be confronted by this vengeful feminine, who would cause her pain and death. Her ego would be "killed" by her own instinctual self, though the penetrating of her eyes and the experience of ecstasy suggests a spiritual awakening.

What the dream suggests is that the path and the group energy would activate a painful and destructive process. In the dream she was terrified of the needles. If she were to continue on the path she would have to encounter that fear. Her spiritual crucifixion was outlined before her, and she was advised to think carefully before she gave herself to this undertaking. In fact the night she had the dream she had gone to sleep asking for guidance about coming to the group meetings. Her unconscious gave her a clear answer of the "spiritual combat" that she would be choosing if she remained with the group. As Rûmî says:

Acts of spiritual combat are of many kinds, the greatest of which is mixing with companions who have turned their faces towards God and their backs toward this world. No act of spiritual combat is more difficult than to sit with sound companions, for the very sight of them wastes away the ego and annihilates it.[5]

RECLAIMING LOVE

A Sufi group is a place of contradictions in which suffering and joy are bonded together. Underlying everything is the ecstasy of annihilation, the surrender of the ego to the passion of the soul's love affair with God. This love affair is the essence of the path; it is the call and the climax. Each in our own way we are taken into this arena of love. Some of us are tempted by visions of inner beauty, or in a dream by the intimate touch of a lover. Some of us are chased by a haunting and terrifying destiny of desolation, the wind of the spirit that blows across the empty spaces of the Self. It can be the urgency of age that speaks to the seeker and says time is running out, or it can be the deep desire for the ultimate challenge.

When He comes to us we are faced by ourself, by the ego that rises in protest against the coming of the King. The ego knows that its dominance is challenged, and it will fight with every doubt and difficulty. It will continually advise us of the impossibility of the path, of the doubtful nature of surrender, of the loneliness of real love. Distraction after distraction will find its way into our mind or appear in our life. Some seekers are best distracted by self-created problems, others by external challenges that seem more attractive than the daily grind of inner work. Whatever most easily deludes us will come into our life, attracted by the ego which is fighting for its survival.

The work of the lover is just to stay true to the soul's longing for union. Anything that interferes with this inner tryst is an obstacle, and yet every obstacle is an opportunity to come closer to love. Obstacles intensify the feeling of separation and motivate us to go beyond them. Because they are *not that which our heart seeks* they make the heart's desire more conscious. Only if we become lost in the obstacle itself is there the danger of straying from the path, but these are the tests of love.

"The falling is for the sake of the rising." When we are caught in the ego's hall of mirrors there comes the moment of remembrance, the heart's hint. He whom we had forgotten has not forgotten us. In these moments we feel the anguish of our betrayal, the foolishness of our forgetfulness. He whom we love we abandoned. We were waylaid by the ego's cunning and our own blindness. But feelings of failure also belong to the ego. Rather than focus on the pain of letting down our highest aspirations, we must use every effort to reclaim our love, to put aside our problems and call out for help. At these moments when we are breaking away from psychological or mental patterns, it is important that we make every effort to look in a different direction, towards Him whom we love. Otherwise the ego's cunning will capture us again, and the moment for freedom will have passed.

Love does not belong to the mind or the ego. It is His gift and our most direct connection to Him. This is why the energy of love is so potent, "the greatest power of creation."[6] To love Him in the midst of our problems, when we are caught in our delusions, is to step away from the ego towards the Self. We align ourself with the currents of love that run through all of creation and open a door to the wisdom of the heart. The heart has a way of freeing us *from above*. Love dissolves our difficulties because it connects us to a dimension where there are no difficulties. With love as a ladder we can climb out of the ego.

As we move from the mind to the heart we leave behind many of the problems of the ego, but the penance that we pay for love is to have the heart's longing intensified. We learn to suffer the depths of the heart's sadness, and the heart has no limits. Love takes us on a journey which the mind cannot measure, and the suffering of lovers is known only to those who have travelled this path. Because love strips away every illusion, it leaves us naked with nothing to keep us from the soul's hunger for God. There is nowhere to hide and nowhere to run, only the anguish of separation. Separation is humanity's primal pain, and when this pain is not covered with other problems it has a terrible intensity. Often it can seem that the heart is breaking open, for He has said, "I am with those whose hearts are broken for My sake."[7] This is the lane of love which only fools and drunkards enter. Others are wise enough to stay away.

LOVE'S ALCHEMY

Pain and difficulties can help to tear away the veils that separate us from our deepest self. But it is in the innermost chamber of the heart that love's alchemy takes place. Here the soul opens to God, and He impregnates it with His knowledge of Himself. In this mystery the soul is feminine, waiting in a state of surrender for the Beloved to come. The sixteenth-century Indian princess and poet Mirabai knew this mystical truth. Mirabai was devoted to Krishna, her "Dark Lord," and once, when she was wandering in some woodlands sacred to Krishna, a famous theologian and ascetic named Jiv Gosvami denied her access to one of her Dark Lord's temples because she was a woman. Mirabai shamed him with the words: *"Are not all souls female before God?"* Jiv Gosvami bowed his head and led her into the temple.[8]

He whom we love teaches us to love Him. He softens the tissues of our heart and shares with us the passion and the tenderness known only to lovers. He knows the ways of love, the intimacies of the heart's unfolding. Sometimes He seduces us with an inner touch, or He pleads with us to be with Him. For some it is suffering that opens us; for others kind caresses melt away our defenses. Often pain is followed by our yielding to His embrace, or we are awakened to a passion that can itself be frightening because it is beyond our control. With this inner lover there are no boundaries, nor the safety of separation. There is only the surrender of the soul to something so enticing that it can be terrifying, something so vast and endless that we are lost beyond any limits.

For the ego such love is fatal; for the mind it is an execution. For the lover who has surrendered to the needs of the soul the mere hint of this love means more than anything the world can have to offer. The touch of His love within the heart washes away the lover's suffering and anguish, just as the touch of a newborn baby dissolves the pain of childbirth. The soul celebrates His love with the deepest joy that life can bring. It is the song of rebirth, of eternal spring, as *The Song of Solomon* glorifies:

> He brought me to the banqueting house, and his banner over me was love.
> Stay me with flagons, comfort me with apples; for I am sick of love.
> His left hand is under me and his right hand doth embrace me....
> My beloved spake, and said unto me, Rise up my love, my fair one, and come away.

> For, lo, the winter is past, the rain is over and
> gone;
> The flowers appear on the earth; the time of the
> singing of birds is come, and the voice of the
> turtle is heard in our land;
> The tree putteth forth her green figs, and the
> vines with the tender grape give a good
> smell. Arise, my love, my fair one, and come
> away....
> My beloved is mine and I am his: he feedeth
> among the lilies.[9]

He who had seemed so distant, so inaccessible, experienced only through separation, takes the lover by the hand and leads her towards union.

The Song of Solomon is one of the great Western celebrations of mystical love, of the soul's ecstatic delight in the caresses of the Beloved. Yet each of us who walks the path of love knows this same song as the most intimate and personal story. Sometimes it is told in dreams, hinted at by the presence of a waiting lover or by an erotic embrace. In the following dream, the dreamer teaches her inner masculine and feminine how to love each other. She is then free to go to where her real lover is waiting:

> There is a couple who don't know how to
> love each other. I tell the man how she wants to
> be touched. Then I tell the woman how to let
> him touch her. She says, Fine, but he can't touch
> her navel. It is taboo.
> I am then free. It is nighttime. I fly through
> the air arriving in a strange land. I take a dip in
> a crystal-clear pool, which refreshes me inside
> and out. It is like being nourished. Then I walk

on the sand past groups of doors of different colors. I look down and see that my dress changes to these colors as I pass.

I come to a door with a black-and-white pattern. There is only one door like this. I enter, walking on the sand. He is sitting crosslegged, waiting. I look down and see that my dress has lots of small hooks from my neck to my ankles. I begin to unhook them, saying, "I know I can do this." I finish, and taking off my dress I am naked. He turns me over and impregnates me from behind, filling my belly with light. I go and sit and watch a sunset that isn't a sunset, with a red, red sky and earth.

The dream begins with a couple who don't know how to love each other. In our culture the relationship between the masculine and feminine has been so battered and distorted that we usually need to work hard to reclaim the harmony and love that is our natural inner state, the balance of yin and yang. He needs to know how she wants to be touched, for the masculine to be sensitive to the inner needs of the feminine. She needs to let him touch her. The masculine is the dreamer's conscious, assertive self, and the light of consciousness needs to touch the more hidden, feminine, instinctual self, without imposing, but rather allowing, the values of the feminine to become conscious.

Only too easily can the presence of the masculine be a brutal invasion into the feminine qualities of relatedness and wholeness. Only too often does the inner feminine respond with anger and resentment, denying the masculine the feeling of wholeness, alienating him from any connection to the inner meaning of life. The natural state of the feminine is one of undifferentiated wholeness, in which everything is a part of the one great whole of life. The masculine quality of discrimination is necessary in order to communicate the subtleties of the feminine, in order to bring her sense of inner relatedness and natural wisdom into consciousness. Describing the inner masculine as a "torchbearer," Irene de Castillejo says, "In a woman's world of shadows and cosmic truths he provides a pool of light as a focus for her eyes."[10]

In the myth *Eros and Psyche*, which is a tale of feminine individuation, one of Psyche's tasks is to separate out the muddled heap of seeds left her by the goddess. The seeds are the inner potential of the feminine, but in order for this natural potential to be of use it must be separated and ordered—a masculine activity. But Psyche is helped in the impossible task of separating the seeds by ants, who represent an instinctual ordering principle. Eric Neumann, commenting on this story, says that this represents "a development towards consciousness, light, and individuation, but, in contrast with the corresponding development in the male, she *preserves the umbilical cord that attaches her to the unconscious foundation.*"[11]

In the dream, the dreamer teaches the woman how to let the man touch her. She has to learn to be responsive to the masculine, to be open to his quality of clear consciousness. But he cannot touch her navel: "It is taboo." The woman's navel is where the umbilical cord connects her to the Great Mother, where she receives her instinctual nourishment and connection to the wholeness of life. This is a sacred connection which she cannot allow to be touched by the cutting consciousness of the masculine.

The development of masculine consciousness

necessitates separation, which is why in tribal life the boy's initiation into manhood marks the moment when he leaves the women's hut and the world of his mother forever. In contrast the girl remains within the world of the mother as she develops into womanhood. Feminine consciousness retains its connection to the Great Mother and thus has an instinctual wisdom and understanding of the sacred wholeness of life, which the masculine lacks. The violation that many women feel is the result of living in a masculine culture which does not honor this sense of wholeness which the feminine *knows* to be life's foundation. This experience of violation happens at an instinctual level: women *feel* that their umbilical connection has been cut, and yet have no conscious knowledge of what has happened. Possibly the experiences of physical abuse that many women are being forced to confront, rather than repress, mirrors a need for the feminine to bring into consciousness this deep sense of collective violation.

THE NEED FOR BOUNDARIES

But in this dream of love the woman stresses that the man cannot touch her navel. The dreamer honors her own wholeness with an awareness that there are places within her feminine psyche that are not to be shared with the masculine, even in love. This is of tremendous importance, because it is through boundaries that places remain sacred. Our present collective culture has abandoned the sacred and so allows for every violation. The development of our own individuality means taking responsibility for what we each believe to be sacred and preserving our inner boundaries.

At the beginning it is often difficult to value our own sacred inner space, to protect it from negativity or an unsympathetic outer environment. Women can find it particularly difficult to create boundaries because they have an instinctual sense of the relatedness of everything, of life's primal oneness. The act of exclusion, which is an integral part of creating boundaries, goes against the feminine drive to embrace and include. A woman needs to find a way of creating boundaries that is not a violation of her instinctual feeling of wholeness.

The same woman who dreamt about teaching the couple how to touch each other had another dream that pointedly imaged the need to protect a sacred space through exclusion. She dreamed that she is given the keys of her teacher's car, a blue Volkswagen Beetle. She has to drive her teacher to a spiritual retreat and is overjoyed at the opportunity to spend time together with her teacher and be able to ask all the questions she wants. However, just as she is about to get into the car a number of other people arrive, some carrying boxes, who also want to come in the car. The dreamer realizes that there isn't enough room for these people, but nearby is her mother's car. Her mother's car is a big, old-fashioned American car in which there is space for everybody and all the luggage. However, at the end of the dream the dreamer knows that if she takes everyone in her mother's car she will not be able to have the intimate conversation with her teacher that has been offered to her.

The dreamer is given an inner opportunity to travel with her spiritual self, but on this journey there is not room for all aspects of herself, nor for the boxes of her psychological baggage. In contrast, her mother's car symbolizes her feminine conditioning in which there is space for everyone, problems and all. But this conditioning does not allow for any intimacy or opportunity for spiritual dialogue. In order to travel with her teacher the dreamer has to be conscious of her own spiritual needs and exclude all the other aspects of herself who want to intrude or come for the ride. When we discussed the dream the dreamer was asked how she would do this. She replied with simple directness, "Exclude everything that does not belong to the Truth."

This act of exclusion is to realize a state of spiritual poverty in which the wayfarer looks only towards God for fulfillment. If we consciously state to ourself our spiritual needs, and make them an inner priority, we also have to exclude everything which interferes with this focus. Spiritual life is learning to become one-pointed, to honor our desire for Truth above everything else and make a commitment to realize this goal. This is illustrated by the story of a Sufi who had a dream about the ninth-century master, Bâyezîd Bistâmî. In the dream, God said, "Everyone wants something from Me except Bâyezîd. He only wants Me."

THE CRUCIBLE OF THE HEART

To create boundaries is to honor one's inner wholeness and protect it from external contamination. This is necessary in order to "hermetically seal" the container of our own spiritual rebirth. The alchemists referred to this container as the *vas bene clausum*, the "well-sealed vessel." They understood that the process of psychological and spiritual transformation requires an ability to exclude negative or disruptive influences.[12] The process of transformation is only too easily disturbed and the energy needed for the work dissipated.

In the dream the Volkswagen Beetle is blue, which is the color of the feminine. This suggests that there is an aspect of the feminine that allows for spiritual intimacy. While the maternal conditioning lacks the ability to make boundaries, the divine feminine has a quality of devotion that is a one-pointed act of surrender to Him:

> I offer to Thee the only thing I have,
> My capacity of being filled with Thee.

Devotion contains the sword of love that excludes all that is not His will. Devotion is an attitude of the heart that focuses the seeker on what is highest. To bow down before Him is an act of surrender that takes the seeker into the inner chamber of the heart, which is protected by the Self and the energy of love from any negative influence. For the lover the heart is the real alchemical container. It has a purity that does not allow any contamination to take place.

The heart is the place of greatest security and yet also the place of greatest vulnerability. To enter the heart is to be open to the pain of love. The contradictions of the heart are both confusing and painful, but we need to learn to embrace them. Often it is easier to enter the arena of love when we are in a spiritual group which provides us with a protected space. The protected space of the group is a stepping stone to the real security of the heart.

A meditation group is where we come together to honor and come closer to what is sacred within us. This can only happen if we feel safe, if we feel that we are in an atmosphere in which the sacred is protected. Irina Tweedie never called herself a teacher, just "the caretaker of her apartment." She looked after the place where her group met for meditation, allowing nothing to disturb the atmosphere. Furthermore, the energy of love which permeates a Sufi group creates an atmosphere that is in itself a sanctuary.

The sense of security which we experience within the group can also help us to create the boundaries which we need within our own psyche. We feel the freedom and potential for inner work that comes from a protected space. This encourages us in the often painful work of creating inner boundaries. Because we are each unique these boundaries will be different for each of us. Therefore nobody can teach us how to accomplish this, but we are often guided by dreams or by an inner sense that is awakened within the consciousness of the heart.

The path involves the psychological work of creating boundaries and the spiritual work of surrender. The two fundamental practices of the Naqshbandi path, the *dhikr* and the meditation, are designed to help us in this work. The practice of the *dhikr*, the repetition of His name, is in essence an act of devotion in which we give our whole attention to Him. The *dhikr* is a powerful method of excluding what does not belong to Him, both the self-perpetuating activities of our own mind and the distractions of the outer world. Wherever we go, whatever we do, we remember His name and so remain in His presence.

God has promised, "I am the companion of him who recollects Me,"[13] and His companionship is *the greatest* protection from any disturbance. His presence protects us from the illusions of the world and our own ego. The protection given by His companionship is one of affirmation rather than negation. He does not reject His own world, but affirms what is highest within us. In His presence our relationship to Him becomes the central focus of our being. He reminds us of Himself, and even in the multiplicity of the world we recognize the one face of our Beloved. When we say His name the secret of His creation responds. His name is written in every atom, yet this is hidden from ordinary consciousness. As His name resounds within our own being and permeates both the cells of our body and the substance of our soul, so with the eye of the heart we see His name imprinted in His creation.

Creation reveals its hidden face to those who know His name. This is the awakening of the consciousness of the heart, which, unlike the consciousness of the mind, experiences through oneness rather than duality. While the mind experiences only through separation and differentiation, the heart *knows* through unity. In the consciousness of the heart the Creator and the creation are united, and we are a part of this union.

Practicing the *dhikr* we see His face mirrored in His creation, feel His single presence beneath the multiplicity of His world. In meditation we go deep within ourself, away from the outer world and also from our own ego. We discipline ourself to go beyond the mind and the emotions and so protect ourself from their disturbing influence. In the silent meditation of the heart we use the energy of love to silence any disturbances and learn to surrender to Him, whose love permeates us. Meditation gives us access to the inner chamber of the heart where we are infinitely secure. Through the practice of meditation we are able to create a link to the higher levels of consciousness which are not influenced by the collective pressures of the outer world or the desires of the ego. Meditation separates us from the outer world but connects us to a sense of oneness in which love permeates all life. In meditation we take off the shoes of this world and enter into the sacred space of our own Self. In this sacred space we are secure enough to lose ourself to love.

THE COLORS OF LOVE

In the journey towards intimacy with our own inner-most self we need the masculine to create boundaries and to persevere "in spite of everything." The feminine embraces our wholeness and draws us into the arena of love. The feminine holds the secrets of the soul, the mysteries of spiritual conception and birth. Within the womb of the soul the Self gives birth to Itself; the infinite enters into manifestation. Then the eyes of the heart are opened and His hidden face becomes visible through the veil of creation.

In the dream of the couple learning how to love each other, after the couple learns to touch, the dreamer feels free and flies through the nighttime sky. Free from the conflicts of masculine and feminine, free from the need to assert herself or the fear of violation, she is able to enter a different dimension: a strange land where she takes a dip in a crystal-clear pool. To enter the inner sanctum of oneself requires security and vulnerability, an openness to the unexpected and a collapse of self-judgement. Freedom is our real nature but so often we protect ourself from its apparent danger through psychological problems and conflicts.

The dream's pool contains the crystal-clear waters of life, free, unpolluted by the ego and its desires and patterns of self-defense.[14] This is a place of initiation, of a baptism in the waters of the Self. This water refreshes the dreamer inside and out, nourishing her with the purity of her inner being. But initiation is also a commitment, a commitment to serving the Self and not the ego. Service to the Self requires a degree of purification that empties us of everything that would interfere with this work. This purification leads to the poverty of the heart, the state of inner emptiness that allows us to enact His will in the world.

The stages of the soul's unfolding are stages of increasing purification which the Sufis have symbolized as different colors. This process of purification is the "polishing of the heart" in which the energy of love wears away the impurities embedded in the psyche. The "colors" refer to the quality of light that is released in the stages of purification. Only when the heart is totally pure can it reflect the white light of the Self. The density of the ego breaks this single source into different rays, just as a prism creates a rainbow. On the return journey we experience these different qualities of the one light as different aspects of our own essence. For just as we have different aspects of our personality, so are there different aspects of the Self.

He, the unknowable one, is known through His names and attributes: His Mercy, His Justice, His Generosity, His Power, and all His other attributes. We come to know Him as these divine attributes are revealed within our own being. The stations of the path are stages of self-revelation, and because we are made in His image, what is revealed are His qualities. Ibn 'Arabî describes this essential unity of God and man:

> God describes Himself to us through ourselves. Which means that the divine Names are essentially relative to the beings who name them, since these beings discover and experience them in their own mode of being. Accordingly, these Names are also designated as Pres-

ences (Hadarât), that is, as the states in which
the Godhead reveals Himself to His faithful in
the form of one or another of His infinite
names.[15]

He reveals Himself within the heart of His servant. On
the journey beyond all form, the lover experiences
within himself the qualities of the Beloved, the names
of God:

> In traversing the spiritual path, the Gnostic
> passes from station to station, never losing a
> positive attribute after having gained it. One by
> one, in perfect harmony, he assumes the traits of
> the divine names. Having reached the highest
> station, he owns all stations. Having assumed the
> traits of all the divine names, he now manifests the
> name of Allâh itself. Just as Allâh designates
> nothing specific, but rather everything—Being
> and all its attributes—so also perfect man is
> nothing specific, since he is all things. Each station
> of the path represents a specific perfection of
> knowledge and character.... But the Gnostic pos-
> sesses all divine attributes and is delimited by
> none. He appears in each and every situation as
> wisdom requires and the secondary causes de-
> mand....
>
> The people of perfection have realized all
> stations and states and passed beyond these to the
> station above both majesty and beauty, so they
> have no attribute and no description. It was said
> to Abû Yazîd, "How are you this morning?" He
> replied, "I have no morning and no evening;
> morning and evening belong to him who becomes
> delimited by attributes, and I have no attributes."[16]

The lover longs to be lost in God to such a degree that nothing remains. The highest station is "no station." But this process of annihilation is gradual, and as aspects of the ego "die" attributes of the Beloved are revealed. Before we are lost in the nothingness of His presence we come to know His divine names, the qualities of our own divine nature.

The knowledge of the heart comes through oneness, through identification and absorption. In order to realize something within the heart we have to become it, we have to know it as a part of ourself. Thus as the dreamer passes the different doors of different colors, she "changes to these colors." She becomes that aspect of herself, that quality of His light. In coming to know herself she comes to know her Lord.

BEHIND THE DOOR OF THE HEART HE IS WAITING

Finally the dreamer comes to a door with a black-and-white pattern. Black symbolizes the deepest nature of the feminine, the empty inner space that is the real abundance. White is the pure essence of the masculine spirit. Together they point to the primal opposites of creation, the polarities of life. Feminine and masculine, expansion and contraction, yin and yang: from these polarities is born the dance of life.

On the journey towards wholeness the wayfarer is thrown between the opposites, between nearness and separation, between the inner and the outer, between the unconscious and the conscious. Energy is born from the opposites, from the interplay of positive and negative. The friction of the opposites provides the momentum that drives us towards the Self, where the opposites are reconciled. Carl Jung describes the psychological dynamic of this process:

> Ascent and descent, above and below, up and down, represent an emotional realization of opposites, and this realization leads, or should lead, to their equilibrium. This motif occurs very frequently in dreams, in the form of going up- and downhill, climbing stairs, going up or down in a lift, balloon, aeroplane, etc. ... The painful suspension between opposites gradually changes into a bilateral activity of the point in the center. This is the "liberation from the opposites," the *nirdvanda* of Hindu philosophy....[17]

On each stage of the spiral path the process is repeated: again and again the opposites are constellated and then united. Always the mystery deepens and the love intensifies. The goal of the mystic is to go beyond duality into the oneness of His Presence. Just as the name embraces all His names, contains all His attributes, so does the lover lost in the Beloved experience all the opposites reconciled within. To quote Ibn 'Arabî:

> The final and ultimate return of the Gnostics ... is that the Real is identical with them while they do not exist.... The Gnostic is known only through the fact that he brings opposites together, for all of him is the Real. Thus Abû Sa'îd al-Kharrâz was asked, "Through what have you known Allâh?" He replied, "Through the fact that He brings opposites together," for he had witnessed their coming together in himself...."[18]

For the mystic the primal pair of opposites is that of the lover and the Beloved:

> In the whole of the universe there are only two, the lover and the Beloved. God loves His creation and the soul loves God. In order to be able to create, the One Being had to become two, and logically there had to be a difference between the two.... The creation was only possible because of the two opposites.[19]

As the soul gives herself to her Beloved these opposites are brought together in the experience of union. In surrendering to God we allow Him to enact this love affair within us. Suffering has burnt away our resistance and longing has strengthened the heart. The path prepares us for each act of love, for each unveiling. Our dreamer has been purified in the crystal-clear pool of her inner being. She has passed the colored doors reflecting the aspects of her Beloved. Now through the single black-and-white door she walks to Him.

Since the beginning of time the Beloved has been waiting for us to come to Him. Eternally patient, He is always present behind the door of the heart. We come to Him when we are strong enough to bear the intensity of His love, when we are desperate enough to forsake our own self, and when our tears have taught us to be vulnerable. The dreamer undresses before her Beloved, unhooking the many small hooks of her dress. Spiritual nakedness is our gift to God. Freeing ourself from our conditioning and all other attachments we allow our essential poverty to be revealed. This is the poverty of the heart which the lover knows in the moment of surrender. It is a state of openness, emptiness, and dependence. It is the vulnerability of being.

ONLY THE HEART KNOWS

"The being of the lover and Beloved are the same."[20] His heart is within our heart. This is the mystery of union as like attracts like, like merges into like. Naked before God we return to the fire that formed us, that gave birth to the mystery of our own heart. With each meeting we are reborn, transformed by His touch. Only the heart can know what this meeting means. It is the hidden secret of matter and the incarnation of love.

The Beloved impregnates the naked dreamer from behind, "filling my belly with light." His face will always be hidden in the act of love because His beauty would be too terrifying. This is why He comes to us "like a thief in the night," entering unexpectedly in the unknown darkness. Because He comes from behind, from the hidden part of ourselves, our mind and con- sciousness cannot resist His coming. Suddenly the heart knows He is present. Light merges with light. He impregnates His lover with His knowledge of Himself. "None knows God but God," but in the heart of His servant His light illumines Himself.

His impregnation of His lover dissolves the bound- aries between the two. The child conceived within the womb of love is unity, the conscious awareness of His eternal presence. In the inner chamber of the heart we know and experience the tremendous unity of lover and Beloved: "I am He whom I love, He whom I love is me." In the outer world we are given the gift of recognizing that same unity mirrored in the creation: "Wheresoever you turn, there is His Face."[21] The glimpse of unity is His gift to those who love Him. The more we surrender ourself to the pain of His presence, the more we burn with the anguish of longing, the more we empty the crucible of the heart of all traces of duality:

> Not until TWO has been erased
> will lover enjoy Union with Beloved.[22]

Al-Hallâj, who made this statement, knew that complete unity could only be realized through physical death. His final utterance on the gallows was, "It is enough for the lover that he should make the One single."[23] While we remain alive we will always remain separate, as a servant to our Lord, but inwardly we can be lost in the ocean of love's unity.

HELD IN THE HEART OF GOD

What was more pleasing in the world than when
The lover went with lover, the friend with friend.
The rest was only grief, while that was all joy.
The rest was only talk while that was all deed.

Abû Sa'îd ibn Abî-l-Khayr[1]

IGNITING THE SPARK OF LONGING

The spiritual path begins when God looks into the heart of His servant and infuses it with divine love. This is the moment of *tauba,* or repentance, which the Sufis call "the turning of the heart."[2] With His glance of love the Beloved touches the heart of the seeker. In that moment the inner door of the heart opens and the heart experiences His love for us, which awakens our love for Him. "We love Him because He first loved us," Saint John says in his epistle (4:19). This awakening of the heart brings into consciousness the inner bond of love that unites the Creator and His creation.

In this experience of awakening we know that He holds the heart of His servant in His heart. This is not a mental knowing, but a knowing of the heart. It is a revelation of love's oneness—a momentary awareness of our primordial state of oneness with God. He awakens the remembrance of the heart, a remembrance that does not belong to time, but to the eternal moment of the Self. This is the Call of the Beloved that seduces the lover, that turns him away from the world to begin the long and painful journey Home.

The glance of the Beloved ignites the divine spark within the heart, creating the fire that will burn away the veils of separation, the coverings of the Self. Abû Saʻîd says that God places a "living and luminous fire in the breasts of His servants in order that their 'self' (*nafs*) may be burned." This fire becomes the fire of longing which never dies, "neither in this world nor in the next."[3] The Beloved "produces a need and longing in man's heart; then He contemplates that need and sorrow, and in His bounty and mercy deposits in that heart a spiritual substance.... That substance is called *sirr Allâh*.... It is immortal and does not become naught, since it subsists in God's contemplation of it."[4] *Sirr Allâh* is the "consciousness of God,"[5] which God communicates to the hearts of His servants.

The fire of longing is born from the glance of God, a glance which contains His consciousness of His Own Unity. The pain born from His glance is the knowledge of union which inflames the feeling of separation. In the center of his pain of separation the lover knows that he is always united with his Beloved. The cry of the soul comes from the remembrance of love's eternal moment, the soul's union with the Beloved. The paradox of love is that we are both united and separate. The awakening to oneness is also an awakening to the pain of separation. Love draws us back to ourself with the pain of incarnation, which is the separation of the soul from its source.

The awakened heart knows that it is loved beyond measure. This knowledge confronts us with the emptiness of our exile, with the desolate awareness that here, in this world, His face is hidden. Yet at the same time this knowledge of love drives the seeker through the deserts of despair, through the dark night of the soul's separation. In the emptiness created by His absence we are held by the thread of His presence. The journey home is only possible because in the very center of our being, in the innermost chamber of the heart, we are always in His presence. We are held in the heart of God.

Only because we are held in His heart are we able to endure the pain of love. Because our being is aligned with its source we can walk the path of our own destruction. If we were not held, centered in the Self, we could be dangerously unbalanced by the energy of love as it breaks up the attachments and conditioning that imprison us. Love's destruction would be unbearable without His hidden embrace.

CONSENTING TO LOVE

His embrace makes us search for Him and enables us to endure the pain of the search. Our initial offering is that of conscious cooperation with the quest. We need to say, "Yes." The Beloved gave us the gift of free will, and although He calls us to Him we have the freedom to accept or reject this call.

The Sufi says, "It is the consent which draws down the grace." Our consent opens the outer door of the heart that lets the transformative energies of love into our life. Only the Beloved has the key to the inner door of the heart, the door which connects the soul with God. Opening this door He activates the heart of hearts with the energy of His call. When we say, "Yes," when we willingly give ourself to the path, we inwardly open and align ourself with love's call. The greater the commitment, the more fully we surrender to love, the greater the currents of love that can flow from within. Love is the power that destroys, transforms, and unites us. Thus the more love we allow in, the more painful and quick the journey.

Our consent is not just a momentary, single, "Yes," but a state of surrender that needs our constant attention. The doorway of love is easily obscured by the ego and we need to keep vigilant. Inwardly we may remain open and yet the will of the ego distracts us from nourishing our longing. And as the process deepens there are different levels of consent. The demands of love intensify. Continually we need to give ourself to Him and to what He wills. This attitude of constant surrender aligns our consciousness with the deeper dimensions of the heart. Gradually the heart's proximity to God becomes reflected into consciousness, until the mind, the body, the whole being are surrendered in affirmation of His love.

He turns our heart towards Him and we consent. This consent is the conscious recognition that He is the Lord. We incarnate the soul's affirmation, made at the primordial covenant, when in response to His question, "Am I not your Lord?" the "not-yet-created humanity" responded, "Yes we witness it." The journey home is made in remembrance of our eternal commitment to Him. Because we belong to Him, we walk the path of the lover's return, allowing this timeless moment of our original affirmation to be born into consciousness.

When we consent to give ourself to God and to remember Him, we welcome the destiny of the soul. The soul attracts our attention to the particular path, the spiritual tradition that we need to follow. A spiritual path is in essence an orientation of the soul towards God which manifests in its outer form as a specific tradition, with its rituals and practices. These rituals and practices are designed to turn the outer attention of the wayfarer towards the source, and to harmonize his or her human and divine elements. This may be through dance, through prostrations, or through silence. It can be through chanting or pilgrimages, fasting or the sharing of dreams. Different meditation techniques and spiritual exercises suit different types of seekers, depending on the structure and vibration of their inner bodies. We are attracted towards a path or lineage that is in tune with our soul, and whose practices will help us orient ourself towards our true nature.

CLIMBING THE COSMIC MOUNTAIN

When we find the right path the soul rejoices. It has found the nourishment it needs, the energy field that will enable it to fulfill its deepest purpose. In response the soul often gives the conscious self a sign as a confirmation. This can be a momentary glimpse of a spiritual reality, a taste of truth. Sometimes the soul gives a dream that infuses the seeker with the wonder of the quest. The following dream came as a confirmation of the seeker having found the right path, and emphasizes the divine connection that is the center of everything.

> I have climbed to the top of the highest mountain in the world. On the peak it forms a cone, bare-earthed with a large pole coming out of its center. I am told: If I place a feather near the base of this pole, in the earth, it will rotate around the pole to face the opposite direction. I place a large white tail-feather into the ground, and it rotates 180° into its foretold position.

> I now see the entire world, from the top of
> the mountain peak, as contained within a sphere.
> Everything, the earth and the sky, revolves
> around the pole. The sky is filled with a fluid,
> golden color, surrounded by blue.

This dream shows the seeker the whole journey home
that is before him, and the glory of the Oneness that
awaits him. It is filled with archetypal symbolism,
ancient images that belong to the mystical tradition.
The highest mountain in the world is the cosmic
mountain imaging man's highest aspiration. The cosmic mountain is such an important image that it has
been the basis of sacred buildings. The *ziqqûrât* of
Babylonia "typified the cosmic mountain with seven
stories whose colors corresponded respectively to
those of the seven Heavens; thus allowing the pilgrim,
ritually, to climb to the summit, that is, to the culminat-
ing point which is the cosmic north, *the pole round
which the earth revolves.*"[6]

In Islamic mysticism the cosmic mountain is called
the mountain of Qâf which "the exile must climb when
he is summoned at last to return *home*, to return *to
himself.*"[7] The summit of this mountain is where the
pilgrim meets his own divine essence, "the one who
gave birth to him." This inner essence which gives birth
to our quest is our connection to the divine world.
Traditionally, at the summit of the mountain of Qâf is
the *celestial pole*, symbolizing the *cosmic north*, the
spiritual orientation within the human being. The
summit is the threshold that opens into the beyond,
and the *pole,* as the center around which everything
revolves, is analogous to the heart.

Listening to this dream was to hear a timeless story
come alive. The dreamer was a research scientist with

little knowledge of mystical symbolism. But his dream told the soul's most primal tale, that of the return to the center. The spiritual journey that now lay before him was the journey to the inner connection that is found within the heart. This story does not belong to the linear, horizontal framework of temporal evolution, but gives a vertical orientation, an orientation which confers the deepest meaning to life. The cosmic north is found *at the summit of the mountain.* This vertical orientation is the orientation of the heart, which contains the link of love that connects the Creator and the creation.

THE RETURN OF THE EXILE

Arriving at the bare earth at the summit of the mountain the dreamer is told that if he places a feather near the base of the pole it will rotate around the pole to face in the opposite direction. He places a large white tail-feather into the ground, and it rotates 180°. A feather is an ancient symbol of our aspirations. If we place our aspirations into the ground at the center of ourself, this feather will turn to face in the opposite direction, symbolizing the turning away from the world, the turning back to God.

For the Sufi there are three journeys: the journey from God, the journey back to God, and the journey in God. The journey from God is the journey of exile as the soul, born into a body, loses its state of proximity with God. In Sohravardî's *Recital of the Occidental Exile* the child of the Orient is sent into exile in the West, where he is put into chains and thrown into a well, from which he can only escape at night for fleeting moments. He becomes increasingly powerless due to exhaustion and forgetfulness. Then the hoopoe, the mystical guide, brings a message from his family, reminding him of his real home. In the blazing light that is awakened within him, he sets out for the Orient which is not in the east but in the cosmic north, a vertical rather than a horizontal direction. The exile must climb the cosmic mountain of Qâf to the very top, up to the *heavenly pole*.[8]

The return journey begins with the moment of *tauba*, which is a conscious awakening to our state of exile. Then we must climb the cosmic mountain within us in order to reconnect with the dimension of the soul, with the inner realm of the heart. This return journey is a 180° turn, symbolized in the *shahâda, "Lâ ilâha illâ llâh"* ("There is no god but God.") *"Lâ ilâha"* is the negation, the awareness of the illusory nature of this world of exile. Turning away from the outer world and the desires of the ego we look inward, for Truth is only to be found within the heart. The negation is followed by the affirmation, *"illâ llâh,"* in which we affirm the heart's connection to God—that we belong only to Him.

For our dreamer this 180° turn *happens of its own accord* when he places one white feather in the ground near the pole. A white feather as a symbol of man's aspiration for truth is echoed in the story of the Simurgh. When one white feather of this mystical bird landed in China, mankind's spiritual search began. 'Attâr writes that "All souls carry an impression of the image of this feather."[9] In placing the white feather of his aspiration into the ground, the dreamer "earths" his desire for truth near to the center of himself. This is the commitment, the consent that allows the process of transformation to commence.

Then the mystical revelation takes place as the dreamer sees "the entire world contained within a sphere." The wholeness of life is revealed to him. Everything is contained within the sphere of the Self, and it "revolves around the pole," around the center of himself, which is also the center of the cosmos. The Self, "the individual Self and the universal Self, living in the heart ... lesser than the least, greater than the greatest,"[10] is the center of the universe and at the same time contains the universe. Within our heart we contain all of creation. Creation revolves around the axis of love that is the pole of the world. Walking the path of love we return home to this center, to the heart of hearts which contains both the creation and the Creator, for He has said, "Heaven and earth containeth Me not, but the heart of My faithful servant containeth Me."[11]

THE CIRCLE OF LOVE

The dreamer, setting out upon his journey back to God, is given an experience of the goal. "The end is present at the beginning." The return journey is the dynamic activation of the center, of our pre-eternal inner wholeness which contains *everything*. It is the magnetic effect of the pole, the center, that turns the feather 180°, that re-orients us back to God. The closer our state of proximity to the center, the stronger the magnetic pull of the pole and the quicker the process. However, this state of proximity, this nearness, does not depend upon the attitude or effort of the devotee. It belongs to the soul. The spiritual journey is an awakening of a pre-existing state of nearness to God.

On the Sufi path the nearness of the soul to God is reflected in the nearness with the teacher. The love the teacher has for the disciple depends upon this state of nearness:

> Love cannot be more or less for the teacher. For him the very beginning and the end are the same; it is a closed circle. His love for the disciple does not go on increasing; for the disciple of course it is very different: he has to complete the whole circle. As the disciple progresses, he feels the master nearer and nearer, as the time goes on. But the master is not nearer: he was always near, only the disciple did not know it.[12]

The spiritual journey does not belong to the horizontal, evolutionary dimension. The vertical "pole" of the path has a different perspective on "progress." Spiritual progress is realizing a state of nearness to God *that was always there*. "He is closer to us than our very neck vein," and yet we do not know it. When we give ourself to the path we are contained within this state of inner nearness. The more we surrender the more we open and are able to experience His hidden embrace. To quote Rûmî:

> if you desire an embrace
> just open your arms.[13]

The embrace of the Beloved takes us whirling into the eternal dimension of the heart. This embrace is echoed by the teacher. As the representative of the tradition, the teacher holds the disciple in the energy of the path. The teacher is the "pole," the connection between the two worlds through which the energy of love flows into the heart of the disciple. Without the link of love between the teacher and the disciple there can be no transformation. This link belongs to the level of the soul and can be very confusing to the personality.[14] It is an impersonal connection of love which the teacher is duty-bound to honor. Although the disciple can reject the teacher, the teacher *cannot reject* the disciple, unless the disciple does something so unethical as to break this inner connection.

The teacher contains the disciple and the whole group within the heart. The teacher is contained within the heart of his teacher, even if his teacher is no longer physically alive. The transmission of the path, the chain of spiritual superiors, is a containment in love. This dynamic container provides the security that enables the wayfarer to walk into the fire of self-destruction, and so realize his or her own unique nearness to God—the closeness of the soul to the source.

The group also provides an inner embrace which has nothing to do with personal friendship. There is a closeness among those "who love one another for God's sake," that does not belong to the outer world, but carries the invisible strength of lovers who are near to God. This is what made Rûmî cry, "Go, oh heart, go with the caravan. Go not alone over the stages of the way...."

In the company of friends we are held within the circle of love. We are protected, inspired, and infused with the intoxicating dance known only to His drunkards. Meeting in meditation we are outwardly silent and still. Inwardly we are made to spin with the desire of the moth who is drawn to the flame that will extinguish him forever. The group can be a vortex of longing that draws us into the abyss. When the hearts of His lovers cry with the primal cry of the soul a doorway into the beyond is opened. Those who are addicted to love have stepped over the threshold. They have been caught forever in the trap of nothingness, in the emptiness of boundless love. Those who would follow this path of annihilation should go and sit with these vagrants:

> Go to the places where the wine is drunk, drink
>   there day and night.
> At any moment someone addicted to drink may
>   give you to taste
> The very dregs, the remainder of the wine on the
>   bottom of the glass.[15]

One sip of the dregs of this wine is enough to make you lose your head forever. Then you awake into a world where a different light permeates everything, like the golden glow which our dreamer saw at the end of his dream: "The sky is filled with a fluid golden color, surrounded by blue."

A DREAM OF AWAKENING

A spiritual group is contained by love and at the same time contains this divine energy. As a point of light in space the group gives to the world remembrance of the "essence of the divine essence." Centered on the Self, the group helps to align both the individual and the collective consciousness with the "pole" of love, the axis upon which the world turns. The group creates a connection to our forgotten and rejected inner self, and infuses collective consciousness with the fragrance of our real nature.

Individually and collectively we share the dream of another dimension, the real, eternal world of the Self. Some are haunted by this dream as a memory of a mythical paradise, a golden age of completeness that seems forever lost. The same dream obsesses others in the guise of romantic love, or the fantasies of success or unlimited wealth. These are the projections that capture our attention, the shadows thrown by something unattainable and infinite.

But from behind these illusions the imprisoned, exiled soul calls to us with mankind's most essential dream, "the journey home." This primal dream carries the pain of homesickness and the wonder of total fulfillment. For those prepared to pay the price it is the one thing worthwhile:

> in the end
> a man tires of everything
> except heart's desiring
> soul's journeying[16]

The soul's journey means to live life to its utmost and to awaken out of the shadows of ourself. When we live this dream we carry it into our everyday life where it touches others in ways we will never know, as a friend was shown one night:

> A man is sitting hunched over with his eyes tightly closed. Suddenly something jars him from the side and his eyes pop open. He closes them tightly against the shock, but realizing he has seen something, slowly opens them again. He is seated in a green grassy meadow, surrounded by other seated figures whose eyes are also tightly shut. In the midst dances a beautiful

woman. It was she who bumped into him. Taking in the beautiful meadow, the arching blue sky, he soon finds himself on his feet, dancing. As he forgets himself in the dance he runs smack into a woman, whose eyes pop open for just an instant....

Spiritual awakening is a state of being which has a dynamic effect upon life itself. The awakened spark within the heart goes where it is needed and helps to keep alight the world's fire of spiritual desire. When we live from our own center, our life becomes charged with the frequency of the Self which *is a state of harmony with the wholeness of life.* Our inner life and our outer life are both infused with this higher frequency, which, because it is in harmony with life, is mostly invisible and undetected. We live life in its fullness and we give this fullness to life. This quality of completeness affects our environment. The sense of unity we experience through this balances the collective feeling of fragmentation that dominates our outer world.

Living ordinary life we give to the collective our knowledge of His all-embracing love. This knowledge seeps through the cracks in the patterns of defense constructed by the collective. These defenses are designed to keep the *status quo* of material values, the established ego-goals of our culture. But there is an underlying hunger for wholeness, a need for inner values unpolluted by the ego or material greed. The knowledge of an inner reality feeds this hunger *from within.* There is no need to proselytize or convert, but just to be oneself. This nakedness of being has the most powerful and beneficial effect upon the collective. It helps align the world to its inner core, to the pole of the Self.

Being ourself we defy the collective taboo which says, "Thou shalt not be thyself." This allows for a freedom not of "self-expression" but of self-realization. Silently stating this freedom has the effect of giving permission to others to take the same dangerous step. Individually one influences the collective with the liberating resonance of the Self. But when a group shares this inner orientation its influence is many times more powerful. The group is a protected space to help those who attend its meetings, and it is also an influence on the environment, freeing some of the restrictive patterns of collective conditioning.

TAKEN TO GOD BY GOD

Travelling the soul's lonely path we are carried along by the currents of love that flow from the Beloved. Following the heart's one dream we make our contribution to life and to the world. We live from the essence and bring that essence into our life, where it influences and nourishes our surroundings. But the heart's call is always to a deeper reality than the outer world. We look inward towards a different horizon, into the empty space of the infinite. On this journey the only boundary is the ego, which we cannot pass on our own. We have to be taken beyond ourself:

> He who says he has attained God, has not,
> While he who says he has been taken to God,
> Has indeed attained union with God.[17]

The path contains us, the group supports us. Held within the energy of the tradition we are prepared; we face our darkness and are purified. The teacher is a guide, pointing us ever deeper, keeping the longing within the heart burning until it has consumed everything that separates us from Him whom we love. But finally all must be left behind; there is no path, no group, and no teacher. Every attachment must fall away, every image dissolve.

Into the silent emptiness we are carried by God alone. He is our only friend, our only love. His formless presence is our only companion. He takes back to Himself whom He will, those who are His bondsmen, who have lost everything through their love for Him. With infinite tenderness He takes us beyond our own fear of the unknowable nothingness. He carries us into the bliss of His presence where we do not exist:

> In some state of consciousness beyond dreaming I knew I was merging with the One. I could feel myself being gently pulled out of myself, moving towards some vast ocean of ineffable bliss. Something in me resisted, because I was afraid, but it was only the vestige of fear. Suddenly I felt a pair of vast but incredibly gentle hands underneath me, and they pushed me onwards with such tenderness that it was impossible to resist. I saw nothing, only an impenetrable blackness which was yet suffused with some unseen light, and I realized that I could not merge with this of my own will, that at the final stage those vast gentle hands come to push you gently into the blackness, and all you have to do is surrender totally to that infinite love which wants only to draw you to Itself.

Notes

INTRODUCTION, pages ix-xiv

¹ *Mathnawî* II, 2235-6, trans. Camille and Kabir Helminski, *Rumi Daylight*, p. 156.
² *Katha Upanishad*, trans. Shree Purohit Swami and W.B. Yeats, bk. 2:1.
³ Quoted by Louis Massignon, *The Passion of al-Hallâj*, vol. 2, p. 426.
⁴ *St. Matthew*, 18:20.

THROUGH A GLASS DARKLY, pages 1-20

¹ *First Epistle of Paul to the Corinthians*, 13:12.
² *St. John*, 14:6.
³ Quatrain 388, trans. John Moyne and Coleman Barks, *Open Secret*, p. 8.
⁴ Quoted by Massignon, p. 614.
⁵ Unpublished lecture, Mystics and Scientists Conference, Wrekin Trust, 1985.
⁶ Llewellyn Vaughan-Lee, *The Lover and the Serpent*, pp. 95-96.
⁷ A Prophetic tradition, quoted by Javad Nurbakhsh, *Sufi Symbolism*, vol. 1, p. 126.
⁸ Al-Hallâj, quoted by Massignon, vol. 1, p. 285.
⁹ *The Conference of the Birds*, p. 106.

BEING TOGETHER IN REMEMBRANCE, pages 21-39

¹ Quoted by William Chittick, *The Sufi Path of Love*, p. 159.
² *The Republic*, part 7, bk. 6.
³ Quoted by R.S. Bhatnagar, *Dimensions of Classical Sufi Thought*, p. 54.
⁴ Rûmî, quoted by Chittick, *Sufi Path of Love*, p. 339.
⁵ Television interview, 1988.
⁶ Qur'an, 7:171.

⁷ *Daughter of Fire,* pp. 2-3.

⁸ Trans. Daniel Liebert, *Rûmî, Fragments, Ecstasies,* Poem 7, p. 16.

⁹ Al-Hallâj, quoted by Massignon, vol. 2, p. 226.

¹⁰ Rûmî, trans. Peter Lamborn Wilson and Nasrollah Pourjavady, *The Drunken Universe,* p. 105.

¹¹ Quoted by Massignon, vol. 1, p. 614.

¹² Quoted from Jonathan Star, *Two Suns Rising, A Collection of Sacred Writings,* p. 159.

¹³ The author has discussed in detail the process of projecting the Higher Self onto the teacher in *The Call and the Echo,* pp. 132-40.

¹⁴ Lahiji, quoted by Henry Corbin, *The Man of Light in Iranian Sufism,* p. 118.

¹⁵ T.S. Eliot, "Little Gidding," ll. 253-254.

¹⁶ *Psalm,* 36:9.

¹⁷ Rûmî, trans. Coleman Barks, *Delicious Laughter,* p. 11.

TURNED ON THE POTTER'S WHEEL, pages 40-58

¹ Quoted by Massignon, vol. 3, p. 99.

² Maghrebî, trans. Nurbakhsh, *Sufi Symbolism,* vol. 1, p. 21.

³ *Memories, Dreams, Reflections,* p. 218.

⁴ Told by Helen Luke, *The Inner Story,* pp. 6-7.

⁵ Trans. Star, p. 132.

⁶ The Sufi master Bhai Sahib says that on the path one is tested until one thinks: "'what can happen—I cannot more than die—' and one accepts it, then the test has been passed and one is ready for the high stage." (Irina Tweedie, *Daughter of Fire*, p. 475; see also Vaughan-Lee, *Call and the Echo*, p. 68.)

⁷ Star, p. 134.

⁸ Bahâ ad-dîn Naqshband describes how his inner relationship with al-Hakîm at-Tirmidhî had this effect: "He had no feature and now I have no feature." See Vaughan-Lee, *Call and the Echo*, p. 148.

⁹ Quoted by Bhatnagar, p. 139.

¹⁰ Trans. Liebert, Poem 22.

¹¹ Corbin, *Man of Light*, p. 100. See also Llewellyn Vaughan-

Lee, *The Bond with the Beloved*, pp. 92-93.
[12] Quoted by Bhatnagar, p. 132.
[13] *St. John*, 3:8.
[14] Mahmud Shabistarî, quoted by Bhatnagar, p. 116.

DOORKEEPERS OF LOVE, pages 59-85

[1] Trans. Coleman Barks, *One-Handed Basket Weaving*, p. 108.
[2] Quoted by Massignon, vol. 3, p. 42.
[3] Quoted by William Chittick, *The Sufi Path of Knowledge*, p. 154.
[4] Rûmî, trans. Coleman Barks, *Like This*, p. 51.
[5] Qur'an, 7:171.
[6] Quoted by Massignon, vol. 4, p. 426.
[7] See Vaughan-Lee, *Bond with the Beloved*, p. 37, for a description of how groups of His lovers are forming dynamic centers of light that are part of a map made of points of light around the world.
[8] The eight basic principles are: 1) "awareness in breathing," 2) "watching over one's steps," 3) "internal mystical journey," 4) "solitude in the crowd," 5) "recollection," 6) "restraining one's thoughts," 7) "to watch one's thought," and 8) "concentration on God." (Annemarie Schimmel, *Mystical Dimensions of Islam*, p. 365.)
[9] See Vaughan-Lee, *Bond with the Beloved*, pp. 116-117.
[10] Told by J.G. Bennett, *Masters of Wisdom*, pp. 146-147.
[11] Quoted by Vaughan-Lee, *Bond with the Beloved*, p. 98.
[12] H. Smith, *The Religions of Man*, p. 212, slightly adapted.
[13] *Collected Works*, vol. 9i, para. 686.
[14] Annemarie Schimmel, *As Through a Veil, Mystical Poetry in Islam*, p. 76.
[15] See Vaughan-Lee, *Lover and the Serpent*, pp. 69-70.
[16] Robert Lawlor, "Dreaming the Beginning," Parabola, Summer 1993.
[17] Quoted by T.C. McLuhan, *Touch the Earth*, p. 99.
[18] A. Stevens, *Archetypes*, p. 265. The two hemispheres of the brain are joined by the *corpus callosum*, which is a bundle of nerve fibres. It is via the *corpus callosum* that the left hemisphere can repress or inhibit the right hemisphere.

Interestingly, women have more fibres in the *corpus callo-sum*, and are thus more able to relate the two sides of the brain.

[19] Lao Tsu, *Tao Te Ching*, trans. Gia-Fu Feng and Jane English, ch. 48.

[20] *St. Matthew*, 9:17.

[21] In recent times in the United States the very real fear of being unable to pay the rent or mortgage and ending up on the street has evoked an archetypal shadow figure of the "bag lady" that appears in many people's dreams.

[22] Rûmî, trans. Coleman Barks, *We Are Three*, p. 37.

[23] *Psychological Reflections*, ed. Jolande Jacobi, p. 35.

[24] T.S. Eliot, *The Wasteland*, ll. 22-24.

[25] Lao Tsu, *Tao Te Ching*, ch. 11.

[26] Rûmî, trans. Coleman Barks, *Feeling the Shoulder of the Lion*, p. 2.

[27] Trans. Coleman Barks, *One-Handed Basket Weaving*, p. 80.

[28] Yahyâ ibn Ma'âdh, quoted by Javad Nurbakhsh, *Spiritual Poverty in Sufism*, p. 15.

THE PEOPLE OF THE SECRET, pages 86-107

[1] Quoted by Schimmel, *As Through a Veil*, p. 32.

[2] See Schimmel, *As Through a Veil*, p. 30.

[3] Quoted by Massignon, vol. 1, p. 600.

[4] Quoted by Massignon, vol. 1, p. 606.

[5] Quoted by Massignon, vol. 1, p. 285.

[6] Quoted by Massignon, vol. 1, p. 286.

[7] Quoted by Massignon, vol. 1, p. 278.

[8] Quoted by Massignon, vol. 1, p. 278.

[9] Quoted by Massignon, vol. 1, p. 77.

[10] Quoted by Massignon, vol. 1, p. 610.

[11] Quoted by Massignon, vol. 1, p. 615.

[12] Quoted by Massignon, vol. 1, p. 634.

[13] Quoted by Schimmel, *As Through a Veil*, p. 122.

[14] Quoted by Massignon, vol. 3, p. 116.

[15] *St. John*, 20:15-16.

[16] Hildegard von Bingen, quoted by Matthew Fox, *The Coming of the Cosmic Christ*, p. 37.

[17] Hâfez, quoted by Nurbakhsh, *Sufi Symbolism*, vol. 1, p. 173.

[18] Quoted by Nurbakhsh, *Sufi Symbolism*, vol. 1, p. 70.

[19] Nurbakhsh, vol. 1, p. 82.

[20] Nurbakhsh, vol. 1, p. 55.

[21] Mahmud Shabestari, quoted by Nurbakhsh, vol. 1, p. 45.

[22] Trans. Lex Hixon, *Atom from the Sun of Knowledge*, p. 246.

[23] Al-Hallâj, quoted by Massignon, vol. 3, p. 104.

[24] *St. Matthew*, 7:6. See also Vaughan-Lee, *Bond with the Beloved*, p. 85.

[25] Al-Hallâj, quoted by Schimmel, *As Through a Veil*, p. 32.

[26] Quoted by Bhatnagar, p. 58.

[27] Johan G.T. Ter Haar, "The Naqshbandî Tradition in the Eyes of Ahmad Sirhindî," *Naqshbandis*, p. 89.

[28] Quoted by Massignon, vol. 3, p. 406.

[29] Rûmî, trans. Coleman Barks, *Birdsong*, p. 36.

[30] *The Cloud of Unknowing*, quoted by T.S. Eliot, *Little Gidding*, l. 238.

[31] 'Attâr, trans. Coleman Barks, *The Hand of Poetry*, p. 57.

PRIMORDIAL NATURE, pages 108-138

[1] Trans. Jane Hirshfield, *The Enlightened Heart*, ed. Stephen Mitchell, p. 64.

[2] Quoted by Evelyn Underhill, *Mysticism*, p. 255.

[3] Quoted by Schimmel, *Mystical Dimensions of Islam*, p. 46.

[4] Qur'an, 17:44, quoted by William C. Chittick, *The Sufi Path of Knowledge*, p. 66, (author's italics).

[5] Trans. Jane Hirschfield, *The Enlightened Heart*, ed. Mitchell, p. 104.

[6] Quoted by Chittick, *The Sufi Path of Knowledge*, p. 195.

[7] Qur'an, 24:35.

[8] The alternative source of nuclear energy is fusion, in which two light nuclei combine to form a heavy nucleus. It offers the prospect for cheap energy once a method has been perfected for controlling its reaction. Fusion is the energy source for the sun and the stars, and its development

reflects the possibility of an energy released through union rather than separation.

[9] "The Second Coming."

[10] Gerard Manley Hopkins, "As kingfishers catch fire."

[11] Henry Corbin, *Creative Imagination in the Sufism of Ibn 'Arabi*, p. 257.

[12] Ibn 'Arabi, quoted by Schimmel, *Mystical Dimensions of Islam*, p. 266.

[13] Qur'an, trans. A.J. Arberry, 89:27-30.

[14] *St. Matthew*, 10:36.

[15] The scapegoat figure takes on the responsibility for the rejected shadow qualities of others, often the shadow of the collective. In the Christian tradition Judas is the archetypal scapegoat, selling Christ for twenty pieces of silver.

[16] *Memories, Dreams, Reflections*, p. 205.

[17] Tweedie, p. 200.

[18] Tweedie, p. 451.

[19] Al-Hallâj, quoted by Massignon, vol. 1, p. 614.

[20] *Katha Upanishad*, trans. Shree Purohit Swâmi and W.B. Yeats, bk. 2:1.

[21] *K. al-riyâda wa-adab al-nafs*, trans. Sara Sviri, *The Niche of Light*, unpublished lecture, 1993.

[22] Najm al-Dîn Kubrâ, quoted by Corbin, *The Man of Light in Iranian Sufism*, p. 72. For a fuller explanation, see Sara Sviri, *The Niche of Light*. See also Vaughan-Lee, *The Call and the Echo*, pp. 129-30.

[23] Qur'an, 2:186, trans. by Chittick, *The Sufi Path of Knowledge*, p. 109.

[24] *Dîwân-i Shams-i Tabrîz*, 5990, quoted by Chittick, *The Sufi Path of Love*, p. 241.

[25] *St. Luke*, 1:46.

[26] Al-Hallâj, quoted by Nicholson, *Studies in Islamic Mysticism*, p. 80.

[27] Quoted by Schimmel, *Mystical Dimensions of Islam*, p. 135.

[28] Qur'an, quoted by Corbin, *Man of Light,* p. 109.

[29] Trans. Coleman Barks and John Moyne, *This Longing*, pp. 19-20.

[30] The Blessed John Ruysbroeck speaks of "a melting and dying into the essential Nudity, and all conditions and all the living images which are reflected in the mirror of Divine

Truth, lapse in the Onefold and Ineffable, in waylessness and without reason....This is the dark silence in which all lovers lose themselves." *The Adornment of the Spiritual Marriage*, III:4, quoted by F.C. Happold, *Mysticism*, p. 293.

THE SCIENCE OF LOVE, pages 139-166

[1] Quoted by Mitchell, *The Enlightened Mind*, p. 77.

[2] *Collected Works*, vol. 8, para. 771.

[3] ". . . all the greatest and most important problems of life are fundamentally insoluble. They must be so because they express the necessary polarity inherent in every self-regulating system. They can never be solved, but only outgrown." C.G. Jung, *Collected Works*, vol. 13, para. 18.

[4] "No worst there is none. Pitched past pitch of grief...."

[5] Quoted by Chittick, *Sufi Path of Love*, p. 155.

[6] Tweedie, p. 58.

[7] *Hadîth qudsî* (extra-Qur'anic revelation).

[8] Told by Andrew Scheeling, *For Love of the Dark One, Songs of Mirabai*, pp. 21-22.

[9] *The Song of Solomon*, 2:4-16.

[10] *Knowing Woman*, p. 76. See also Vaughan-Lee, *Lover and the Serpent*, pp. 53-60.

[11] *Amor and Psyche*, p. 96, (author's italics).

[12] Psychologically, the *vas bene clausum* refers to "the need to withdraw projections and to discriminate between what belongs to oneself and what belongs to another, for one can only transform the contents of one's own psyche and the 'intrusion and admixture' of external psychological material leads only to confusion." Vaughan-Lee, *Lover and the Serpent*, p. 54.

[13] *Hadîth qudsî*.

[14] These are the same waters that Saint John saw in his vision: "And he shewed me a pure river of water of life, clear as crystal, proceeding out of the Throne of God and of the Lamb." *The Revelation of St. John the Divine*, 22:1.

[15] Henry Corbin, *Creative Imagination in the Sufism of Ibn 'Arabî*, p. 115.

[16] Ibn 'Arabî, quoted by Chittick, *Sufi Path of Knowledge*, pp. 375-376.

[17] Collected Works, vol. 14, para. 296. See also Vaughan-Lee, *Lover and the Serpent*, pp. 13-16 and Vaughan-Lee, *Bond with the Beloved*, pp. 11-12.

[18] Quoted by Chittick, *Sufi Path of Knowledge*, p.375.

[19] Bhai Sahib, quoted by Tweedie, p.180.

[20] Shâh Ne'matollâh, *Mathnawî*, trans Peter Lamborn Wilson and Nasrollah Pourjavady, p. 96.

[21] Qur'an, 2:109.

[22] Ahmad Ghazâli, *Sultan Mahmud and the Salt Vendor*, trans. Peter Lamborn Wilson and Nasrollah Pourjavady, p. 86.

[23] Quoted by Massignon, vol. 1, p. 613.

HELD IN THE HEART OF GOD, pages 167-182

[1] Quoted in *The Secret of God's Mystical Oneness*, trans. John O'Kane, p. 533.

[2] See Vaughan-Lee, *Bond with the Beloved*, pp. 5-7.

[3] R.A. Nicholson, *Studies in Islamic Mysticism*, p. 55.

[4] Nicholson, p. 51.

[5] "*Sirr*" literally means secret.

[6] Corbin, *Man of Light,* pp. 41-42, (author's italics).

[7] Corbin, *Man of Light,* p. 43.

[8] Corbin, *Man of Light,* p. 23, (author's paraphrase).

[9] *The Conference of the Birds*, p. 13.

[10] *Katha Upanishad*, bk 1:3, 2, trans. Shree Purohit Swâmî and W.B. Yeats.

[11] *Hadîth qudsî.*

[12] Bhai Sahib, quoted by Tweedie, p. 120.

[13] Trans. Liebert, p. 16.

[14] See Vaughan-Lee, *Call and the Echo*, ch. 6, "The Relationship with the Teacher."

[15] Persian poem, quoted by Tweedie, p. 372.

[16] Trans. Liebert, p. 17.

[17] Attributed to Abû'l Hasan Kharaqârî.

Selected Bibliography

Attâr, Farîd ud-Dîn. *The Conference of the Birds*. Trans. C.S. Nott. London: Routledge & Kegan Paul, 1961.

Bennet, J.G. *Masters of Wisdom*. London: Turnstone Press, 1977.

Bhatnagar, R.S. *Dimensions of Classical Sufi Thought*. Delhi: Motilal Banarsidass, 1984.

The Bible, Authorized Version. London: 1611.

Castillejo, Irene de. *Knowing Woman*. New York: Harper Colophon, 1974.

Chittick, William C. *The Sufi Path of Love*. Albany: State University of New York Press, 1983.

—. *The Sufi Path of Knowledge*. Albany: State University of New York Press, 1989.

Corbin, Henry. *Creative Imagination in the Sufism of Ibn 'Arabî*. Princeton: Princeton University Press, 1969.

—. *The Man of Light in Iranian Sufism*. London: Shambhala Publications, 1978.

Eliot, T.S. *Collected Poems*. London: Faber and Faber, 1963.

Fox, Matthew. *The Coming of the Cosmic Christ*. San Francisco: Harper & Row, 1988.

Gaborieau, Marc; Popovic, Alexandre et Zarcone, Thierry, eds. *Naqshbandis*. Istanbul: l'Institut Français d'Etudes Anatoliennes d'Istanbul, 1990.

Happold, F.C. *Mysticism*. Harmondsworth, England: Penguin Books, 1963.

Hixon, Lex. *Atom from the Sun of Knowledge*. Westport, Connecticut: Pir Publications, 1993.

Hopkins, Gerard Manley. *The Poems and Prose of Gerard Manley Hopkins*. Harmondsworth, England: Penguin Books, 1953.

Jung, C.G. *Collected Works*. London: Routledge & Kegan Paul.

—. *Psychological Reflections*. Ed. Jolande Jacobi. London: Routledge & Kegan Paul, 1971.

—. *Memories, Dreams, Reflections*. London: Flamingo, 1983.

Khan, Inayat and Barks, Coleman. *The Hand of Poetry.* New Lebanon, New York: Omega Publications, 1993.

The Koran. Trans. A.J. Arberry. New York: Macmillan, 1955.

The Koran. Trans. N.J. Dawood. London: Penguin Books, 1956.

Lao Tsu. *Tao Te Ching.* Trans. Gia-Fu Feng and Jane English. Aldershot, England: Wildwood House Ltd., 1973.

Lawlor, Robert. "Dreaming the Beginning," Parabola, Summer 1993.

Luke, Helen M. *The Inner Story.* New York: Crossroad Publishing Company, 1982.

Massignon, Louis. *The Passion of al-Hallâj.* Princeton: Princeton University Press, 1982.

McLuhan, T.C. *Touch the Earth.* London: Garnstone Press, 1972.

Mitchell, Stephen. Ed. *The Enlightened Heart.* New York: Harper & Row, 1989.

—. ed. *The Enlightened Mind.* New York: Harper Collins, 1991.

Neumann, Eric. *Amor and Psyche.* Princeton: Princeton University Press, 1971.

Nicholson, R.A. *Studies in Islamic Mysticism.* Cambridge: Cambridge University Press, 1921.

—. *The Mystics of Islam.* London: Arkana, 1989.

Nurbakhsh, Javad. *Sufi Symbolism,* Volumes I - IV. London: Khaniqahi-Nimatullahi Publications, 1984-1990.

Plato. *The Republic.* Harmondsworth, England: Penguin Books, 1955.

Rûmî. *Delicious Laughter.* Trans. Coleman Barks. Athens, Georgia: Maypop Books, 1990.

—. *Like This.* Trans. Coleman Barks. Athens, Georgia: Maypop Books, 1990.

—. *One-Handed Basket Weaving.* Trans. Coleman Barks, Athens, Georgia: Maypop Books, 1991.

—. *Birdsong.* Trans. Coleman Barks. Athens, Georgia: Maypop Books, 1993.

—. *Open Secret.* Trans. John Moyne and Coleman Barks. Putney, Vermont: Threshold Books, 1984.

—. *This Longing.* Trans. Coleman Barks and John Moyne. Putney, Vermont: Threshold Books, 1988.

—. *Rûmî Daylight*. Trans. Camille and Kabir Helminski. Putney, Vermont: Threshold Books, 1990.

—. *Rûmî: Fragments, Ecstasies*. Trans. Daniel Liebert. Santa Fe, New Mexico: Source Books, 1981.

Scheeling, Andrew. *For Love of the Dark One, Songs of Mirabai*. Boston: Shambhala, 1993.

Schimmel, Annemarie. *Mystical Dimensions of Islam*. Chapel Hill, North Carolina: University of North Carolina Press, 1975.

—. *As Through a Veil, Mystical Poetry in Islam*. New York: Columbia University Press, 1982.

Star, Jonathan. *Two Suns Rising, A Collection of Sacred Writings*. New York: Bantam Books, 1991.

Stevens, Anthony. *Archetypes*. New York: Quill, 1983.

Tweedie, Irina. *Daughter of Fire, A Diary of a Spiritual Training with a Sufi Master*. Nevada City, California: Blue Dolphin Publishing, 1986.

Underhill, Evelyn. *Mysticism*. New York: New American Library, 1974.

Vaughan-Lee, Llewellyn. *The Lover and the Serpent: Dreamwork within a Sufi Tradition*. Shaftesbury, England: Element Books, 1989.

—. *The Call and the Echo: Sufi Dreamwork and the Psychology of the Beloved*. Putney, Vermont: Threshold Books, 1992.

—. *The Bond with the Beloved: The Mystical Relationship of the Lover and the Beloved*. Inverness, California: The Golden Sufi Center, 1993.

Wilson, Peter Lamborn and Pourjavady, Nasrollah. *The Drunken Universe*. Grand Rapids, Michigan: Phanes Press, 1987.

Yeats, W.B. *Collected Poems of W.B. Yeats*. London: Macmillan, 1933.

Yeats, W.B., trans. (with Shree Purohit Swami). *The Ten Principal Upanishads*. London: Faber and Faber, 1937.

Index

Acknowledgments

For permission to use copyrighted material, the author gratefully wishes to acknowledge: Bantam Books, a division of Bantam Doubleday Dell Publishing Group, Inc., for permission to quote from *Two Suns Rising* by Jonathan Star, translation copyright © 1991 by Jonathan Star; Daniel Liebert, for permission to quote from *Rumi: Fragments, Ecstasies* translated by Daniel Liebert; Khaniqahi-Nimatullahi Publications, for permission to quote from *Sufi Symbolism* by Dr. Javad Nurbakhsh; Maypop Books, for permission to quote from *We Are Three, Birdsong, One-Handed Basket Weaving*, and *Delicious Laughter* translated by Coleman Barks; Omega Publications, for permission to quote from *The Hand of Poetry* translated by Coleman Barks with lectures by Hazrat Inayat Khan; Pir Publications, for permission to quote from *Atom from The Sun of Knowledge* by Lex Hixon; HarperCollins Publishers, for permission to quote from *The Enlightened Heart* by Stephen Mitchell, copyright © 1989 by Stephen Mitchell; Threshold Books, RD4, Box 600, Putney, Vermont 05346, for permission to quote from *This Longing* and *Open Secret* translated by John Moyne and Coleman Barks and *Rumi Daylight* translated by Kabir Helminski; Wildwood House, for permission to quote from *Tao Te Ching* translated by Gia-Fu Feng and Jane English.

LLEWELLYN VAUGHAN-LEE, Ph.D., is the author of *The Lover and the Serpent: Dreamwork within a Sufi Tradition* (1990), *The Call and the Echo: Dreamwork and the Inner Journey* (1992), and *The Bond with the Beloved: The Mystical Relationship of the Lover and the Beloved* (1993). Born in 1953, he has followed the Naqshbandi Sufi Path since he was nineteen. In 1991 he moved from London to northern California, where he now lives with his wife and two children. He lectures throughout the United States and Europe on Sufism, dreamwork, and Jungian psychology.

The Golden Sufi Center is a California Religious Non-Profit Corporation dedicated to making the teachings of the Naqshbandi Sufi Path available to all seekers. For further information about the activities of the Center and Llewellyn Vaughan-Lee's lectures, write to:

The Golden Sufi Center
P.O. Box 428
Inverness, California 94937

(415) 663-8773